E 6

86

DISCARD
DISCARD

D1280139

SHAKESPEARE'S HISTORICAL PLAYS

SHAKESPEARE'S
HISTORICAL PLAYS

S. C. SEN GUPTA

Professor of English
Jadavpur University, Calcutta

OXFORD UNIVERSITY PRESS

Oxford University Press, Ely House, London W.1

GLASGOW NEW YORK TORONTO MELBOURNE WELLINGTON
CAPE TOWN SALISBURY IBADAN NAIROBI LUSAKA ADDIS ABABA
BOMBAY CALCUTTA MADRAS KARACHI LAHORE DACCA
KUALA LUMPUR HONG KONG

© *Oxford University Press* 1964

FIRST PUBLISHED 1964
REPRINTED LITHOGRAPHICALLY IN GREAT BRITAIN
FROM CORRECTED SHEETS OF THE FIRST EDITION
BY WILLIAM CLOWES AND SONS LIMITED
LONDON AND BECCLES
1966

In Memory of My Teacher

SUHAS CHANDRA RAY

Preface

SHAKESPEARE'S 'Histories' have received far less attention
than his 'Comedies' and 'Tragedies'. Although during the last
half century the history play has come into its own as a genre,
modern critics, who have made comprehensive studies of the
subject, have looked upon the 'Histories' either as extensions
of medieval moralities or as mirrors of the Elizabethan concept
of history – very often the two themes overlap – and subordinated
the purely literary significance of these plays to their ethical and
political import. It is necessary to redress the balance, to re-
affirm the purely poetical value of historical drama and to treat
the ten plays from *King John* to *Henry VIII* as works of art and
not as political and didactic treatises. This is my apology for
making one more addition to the enormous bulk of Shakespearian
criticism.

The point of view from which the historical plays have been
studied here is indicated in the two opening chapters, and in
elaborating in the later chapters what I have briefly said in the
first two, I have often had to take up the same situations and
characters, and the basic argument has remained the same all
through. This means that there have been occasional repetitions,
though I hope that even when I have repeated myself I have been
able to bring out a new aspect of a continuous argument.

None can read all that has been written on Shakespeare or
consciously remember all that he has read and made his own. In
the footnotes I have tried to acknowledge my debt to the various
works on which I have drawn, but I feel that I have not been able
to record all my obligations. I take this opportunity of recording
my indebtedness to Professor Geoffrey Bullough's *Narrative and
Dramatic Sources* of Shakespeare, Vols. 3 and 4, which I have
constantly used, and it is from his reprint that I have taken the
excerpts I have quoted from *The Troublesome Raigne of King John*.
Quotations from Shakespeare have been taken from the one-
volume Oxford edition of W. J. Craig.

It is the privilege of a Preface to express gratitude to friends who have given encouragement and assistance. I am particularly thankful to my colleague Mr Haydn Moore Williams, M.A., Reader in English, Jadavpur University, and to my former pupil Mr Barun De, M.A., D.Phil., Associate Professor of History at the Indian Institute of Management, Calcutta, for reading over the typescript and making valuable suggestions and comments. The Index I owe to the assistance of my colleague – and pupil – Mr Jagannath Chakravorty, M.A.

Last, and first, I am grateful to the Delegates of the Clarendon Press and their readers for the care with which they have seen the book through the press.

S. C. SEN GUPTA

Jadavpur University
Calcutta

Contents

CHAPTER ONE

The Substance of Shakespeare's 'Histories'

I

IT MAY be asked whether historical plays can form a separate class in dramatic literature. All literature is fiction, and the historical playwright takes so much liberty with his materials – the exigencies of the theatre compel him to be even more drastic than the historical novelist – that the mere fact that some of the incidents and characters had their counterparts in reality does not affect their basic fictional quality. On the other hand, if a historical drama – or a historical novel – is a faithful transcript of the past, it will be more history than literature. Secondly, historical literature which represents particular individuals living in particular epochs cannot have the universal significance we demand of the creations of the imagination. The distinction drawn by Aristotle between poetry and history – the statements of poetry are of the nature of universals and those of history are singulars – may be extended to fictional literature which follows history in its outlines even if it departs from facts in details, for such literature, too, is about particular persons who lived at a particular time and in a particular place.

Did Shakespeare himself want to make a separate genre of his historical plays? The titles of *Richard II* (Quarto) and *Richard III* (Quarto and Folio) describe them as tragedies. *Henry V* is, indeed, called a chronicle history and *Henry VIII* a history, but the Quarto (the first issue of it as well as the second) of *Troilus and Cressida* is also called a history, though it is less historical than *Timon of Athens* and much less so than either *Julius Caesar* or *Antony and Cleopatra*. Heminge and Condell, however, who could not have been unaware of all this, called the ten plays dealing with English kings 'histories' and placed the Roman plays, and also

King Lear, Macbeth and *Cymbeline*, which, like the English historical plays, were derived from Holinshed, among the tragedies. The principle of classification adopted in the First Folio is not without its point, and Heminge and Condell may have had the support of Shakespeare himself, for after the Armada writing plays on themes derived from English history became a craze, and Shakespeare either followed a popular fashion or was in the van of it. We know, further, that Tudor monarchs tried to inculcate a particular view of history, and Shakespeare, it is sometimes said, only dramatized what the historians propounded in their chronicles. In a sense these plays were even more historical than the chronicles, many of which failed to draw a distinction between legend and history. In the ten plays classified as 'histories', the incidents do not concern remote and legendary figures such as Lear and Cymbeline[1] but English kings and barons whose actions formed part of authentic history. And although Shakespeare modifies historical data in his English history plays, here he does not take such liberties as in *King Lear* or *Macbeth*. Referring to Shakespeare's modification of his sources in *Macbeth*, a critic has remarked that Macbeth in history was a good man, and Shakespeare's play shows what genius can make of history! One could not say the same of Richard III, an incredible monster, but no invention of Shakespeare who only transferred him from chronicle to drama. Even in *King John*, although Shakespeare makes large modifications, he does not manipulate history in the manner of John Bale, who makes a Protestant martyr of a cowardly villain.

From yet another point of view, these ten plays may be said to form a separate category which is best named 'history', for even if we do not accept the thesis that here Shakespeare wants to mirror the political problems of his own time or the Tudor interpretation of history, there is no doubt that these plays reflect certain definite periods of English history, which sets them apart from other plays in the canon. *Hamlet* could have been written only by a dramatist of the English Renaissance, but the incidents might have happened at any time and Elsinore might be any place in the world. The same thing may be said of the comedies, and also of *King Lear* and *Macbeth*. In *Othello*, the only assumption we have to make is that the heroine is a white woman in love with a

---

[1] Wilson Knight (possibly alone of all critics) looks upon *Cymbeline* 'mainly as an historical play' (*The Crown of Life*, p. 129), on the ground that it delves into the historic origins of the English nation.

man of a coloured race – black or brown – and beyond that it is not necessary to know who are the men of royal siege from whom Othello fetched his life and being or to enquire into the moving accidents by flood and field, which he passed through before coming to Venice. The plots of *Julius Caesar*, *Coriolanus*, and *Antony and Cleopatra* seem to be firmly rooted in history, but except partly in *Coriolanus* the historical background has little to do with the significance of these dramas. Indeed, these Roman plays are not derived from any historian but from Plutarch, who, although he might have given 'essential history', was a literary artist with a didactic purpose rather than a historian. The very scheme of his biographies, his drawing parallel portraits of people far removed from each other, shows that he was interested more in universal moral significance than in local colour. Shakespeare was more concerned about problems of character than about morals, but in the Roman plays he too uses the historical background only to draw out meanings that are independent of history. Even in *Coriolanus* he wants primarily to reveal the tortured workings of impulses and not to transcribe a slice of Roman history.

This is not the impression produced by the historical plays. The two tetralogies cover a definite period – from 1398 to 1485 – and the story is continued after a brief interval in *Henry VIII*, which reproduces events not far off from Shakespeare's own time. *King John* relates to a more remote period, and it is less historical than the other plays in this genre. Nevertheless the story of King John, who attempted a breach with Rome, had a special appeal for Elizabethan England, and in spite of a highly wayward treatment of the sources this drama in spirit and substance produces an impression of historicity. Of the ten plays, nine are about medieval England, and although they are not devoid of universal significance, that significance is rooted in the particular periods which they represent. One prominent feature of all these histories is their largeness. There are generally more speaking parts in a 'history' than in a comedy or a tragedy and the characters are drawn from all shades of life. What is more, the historical plays – *King John* and the two tetralogies – give us the spirit and atmosphere of medieval England as visualized by an Elizabethan dramatist. The interposition of a particular point of view involves the risk of over-simplification, and it may be questioned if a dramatist who omits the Magna Carta from the story of King John and who gives a caricature of Lollardry in Sir John Falstaff can be said to have portrayed the Middle Ages in all their richness and complexity. Indeed, Bernard Shaw goes to the opposite extreme when he says:

> 'Now there is not a breath of medieval atmosphere in Shakespeare's histories. His John of Gaunt is like a study of the old age of Drake. Although he was a Catholic by family tradition, his figures are all intensely Protestant, individualist, sceptical, self-centred in everything but their love affairs, and completely personal and selfish even in them. His kings are no statesmen: his cardinals have no religion: a novice can read his plays from one end to the other without learning that the world is finally governed by forces expressing themselves in religions and laws which make epochs rather than by vulgarly ambitious individuals who make rows.' (Preface to *Saint Joan*)

This is an exaggerated statement, and like all exaggerations it is misleading. Shakespeare's account of John of Gaunt in *Richard II* is indeed too sympathetic and takes no notice of Gaunt's errors and failures. But it is very similar to and may have been derived from Froissart's account, and since Froissart lived for some time in the Court of Edward III and Richard II it will not be true to say that such a portrait, although imbued in Shakespeare's drama with Tudor patriotism, is unmedieval in spirit. One is free to hold that not one of Shakespeare's kings, not even Henry V, is a statesman, but they may all the same be true representatives of the medieval idea of kingship. The charge of lack of religion is subtler and has to be examined in greater detail. Shakespeare portrays a number of Cardinals – Pandulph, Beaufort, Bourchier, and Wolsey who, of course, belongs to the Renaissance rather than to the Middle Ages – and the Archbishop whom Henry V consults is the highest dignitary of the English Church. These princes of the Church, it must be admitted, are politicians rather than pious men. Shakespeare does not portray the mysticism or the humble piety of medieval Christianity, neither does Shaw. But it does not follow that Shakespeare fails to represent other aspects of the religion of the Middle Ages. Although the medieval religious outlook was other-worldly, the medieval Church made tall claims of suzerainty over all temporal authority and Pope Innocent III was as much a representative of the Middle Ages as St Thomas Aquinas or St Francis of Assisi. It is this aspect of medieval Catholicism which is portrayed in its successive phases in Shakespeare's plays. Cardinal Pandulph is a legate of Pope

Innocent III who raised the Papacy to the height of political power, and as a faithful servant of this masterful Pope he treats the secular authority of kings as subservient to the Church; he first ex-communicates John and then, after extorting abject submission, proceeds to disarm the opposition arrayed against the royal scape-grace. From the days of John to those of Henry IV and Henry V there is a gap of more than two centuries, and we find that from the position of a dictator the priests have descended to that of advisers who comfort, warn and occasionally rebel. In *Richard II*, the Bishop of Carlisle gives a stern warning to Bolingbroke when Richard is deposed, but his argument is based not on the supremacy of the Church but on the inviolability of the king's authority:

> Would God that any in this noble presence
> Were enough noble to be upright judge
> Of noble Richard! then, true noblesse would
> Learn him forbearance from so foul a wrong.
> What subject can give sentence on his king?
> And who sits here that is not Richard's subject?
>
> (IV. i. 117–22)

At this stage the Pope's authority is not challenged, but he is regarded as an alien power who might prove a source of danger to the English crown. When Winchester is made a Cardinal, the Duke of Exeter reminds us in an aside that:

> Henry the Fifth did sometime prophesy, –
> 'If once he come to be a cardinal,
> He'll make his cap co-equal with the crown'.
>
> (1 *Henry VI*, V. i. 31–33)

In *Richard III*, Cardinal Bourchier and the bishops play a very ignoble part; they are pawns in Richard's nefarious game and only show how subservient the Church has become when a powerful and unscrupulous king is on the throne. We have travelled a long way since the days of King John and even of King Henry V. In *Henry VIII*, Cardinal Wolsey figures as the last great ecclesiastic who fixes his ambition on Rome and is crushed by the king whom he wanted to serve and control. Here we are in Renaissance England and on the threshold of the English Reformation. If we trace the progress of Shakespeare's Cardinals from Pandulph to Wolsey and of English kings from John to Henry VIII, we get a glimpse of the emergence of English national-ism and a vivid picture of a very significant aspect of the transition from the medieval world to the modern. Here, indeed, we can visualize the forces, which, lying behind the rows made by vulgarly ambitious men, effect a change from one epoch to another. That is the true function of historical drama as distinct from chronicles or chronicle plays.

II

There are critics who think that the distinction between the 'history play' written by Shakespeare and the top people, and the 'chronicle play' of journeymen is unnecessary. 'It is more useful', says Reese, 'to regard as a history play any that however partially or inexpertly, handled past events in a serious political spirit'. For such critics the distinction between other men's political plays and those written by Shakespeare 'is rather one of quality than of kind'.[1] But whether of quality or of kind, there is, indeed, a vast difference between the chronicle play and Shakespeare's 'histories'. We need not enter here into the controversy whether Shakespeare found writing historical plays a fashion and followed it or whether he himself set the fashion and others took it up. Even F. P. Wilson admits that *The Famous Victories of Henry the Fifth* is anterior to Shakespeare's work in this branch of drama,[2] and we may make the same assumption about the priority of *The True Tragedie of Richard the third*. An examination of these two plays will be enough to show the difference between the chronicle play and the new genre evolved by Shakespeare. The anonymous playwrights who recorded the careers of Henry V and Richard III were anxious above everything else to report as many episodes as could be compressed within two hours' traffic of the stage. Not that there is no emphasis on the main characters, however crudely these might be drawn. Henry V is a heroic figure; and Richard III is a villain built on the grand scale, a monster without scruples but with a conscience which makes him very human. Yet the dramatists are not primarily concerned to reveal the deeper and subtler shades of their characters; they hurry on from incident to incident, condensing in *The Famous Victories* episodes which supplied Shakespeare with plots for three whole plays and amassing in *The True Tragedie* materials only a fraction of which

---

[1]M. M. Reese, *The Cease of Majesty: A Study of Shakespeare's History Plays* (London, 1961), p. 88.
[2]F. P. Wilson, *Marlowe and Early Shakespeare* (Oxford, 1955), p. 106.

Shakespeare could make use of in *Richard III*. The similarity between *The True Tragedie* and *Richard III* is so striking that some
critics look upon the former as a vamped version of the latter. But
the anonymous play, which must have been one of Shakespeare's
source-books, elaborates the episode of Mistress Jane Shore who
is only mentioned in *Richard III*, and gives elsewhere a large slice
of English history from the death of Clarence to the defeat of
Richard III at Bosworth Field, relying on such characters as Page,
Boy, and Report. Shakespeare does include certain incidents not
mentioned in *The True Tragedie* and also elaborates others which
are passed over in the older play. But it is not by comparing
details here and there that we can find the basic difference between
them. What is important is that in Shakespeare's *Richard III*,
although it is an early play, incidents, numerous as they are, have
no importance of their own but are subordinated to the portraiture of character and the organization of the play as an aesthetic
structure. In *The True Tragedie*, although Richard III is powerfully
portrayed and the Jane Shore episode is made the basis of a moral
homily, the total impression is of a string of incidents loosely
connected through character and idea.

The present study proceeds on the assumption that the greatness of Shakespeare consists chiefly in his ability to create men
and women, who, if not imitations of reality, have the vividness
of living characters. In the historical plays Shakespeare succeeds
in endowing the dead skeletons of history with flesh and blood,
and also in creating, with or without suggestions from history,
new characters that are more real than living men. This aspect
of Shakespeare's genius will be dealt with in greater detail later
on. What is relevant in the present context is an enquiry into the
central idea – moral, political or dramatic – which may be said
to emerge from the whirl of incidents and the crowd of characters.
By the time Shakespeare came to handle historical materials,
histories and historical poems – and plays – were being written
with the definite purpose of inculcating what has been called the
Tudor historical myth. It is often thought that Shakespeare's
historical plays are also essentially homiletic, that they are an
elaborate discourse on the duties of kingship and the dangers of
civil dissension. Tillyard, for example, says that Shakespeare was
among the select few who saw a dramatic and philosophical
pattern in the period covering the Wars of the Roses, and he is
thus to be distinguished from those who saw it as a welter of

misery and a rich repertory of lessons on the fickleness of fortune and the chastisement of peccant individuals.[1] Many other critics think that Shakespeare's histories were a mirror of the politics of his own day. Lily B. Campbell points out that there is, indeed, a dividing line between ethics and politics, and 'it is to this distinction between private and public morals, that we must look for the distinction between tragedy and history. Tragedy is concerned with the doings of men which in philosophy are discussed under *ethics;* history deals with the doings of men which are discussed under *politics*'.[2]

Although most people think – and rightly think – that the historical plays deal primarily with the fortunes of princes, the art of government and the doings of men which are discussed under politics, yet there are others who seem to hold that the dividing line between politics and ethics mentioned above is not easy to draw and that patterns of the old morality play with its emphasis on private morals survive in all the historical plays, most notably in the two parts of *Henry IV*. It is contended that much as Elizabethan drama owes to foreign influences and the original genius of the dramatists, it is largely a continuation of native English drama beginning with the cycle plays, and some have gone so far as to hold that the morality structure is deeply embedded in Shakespearian tragedy and comedy. In Dover Wilson's view, '*Henry IV* was certainly intended to convey a moral. It is in fact Shakespeare's greatest morality play'.[3] The essence of the morality play is that man is confronted with a choice between good and evil, he is tempted by the forces of Evil and then is saved from imminent disaster by his own virtues or by the mediation of some super-human power. According to Dover Wilson, Shakespeare symbolizes Vanity in Falstaff, anarchic old world Chivalry in Hotspur and the Rule of Law and the new ideal of service to the state in the Lord Chief Justice. The technical centre of the play is thus not the fat knight but the lean Prince, who links the revelry of East-cheap with the serious affairs at Westminster, and who finally abandons vanity for government. It has been suggested that Richard III is lineally descended from the medieval Vice who was both a clown and a villain.[4]

---

[1]E. M. W. Tillyard, *Shakespeare's History Plays* (Peregrine Books, 1962), p. 59.
[2]'*Shakespeare's "Histories"* ' (Huntington Library, 1958), p. 17.
[3]J. Dover Wilson, *The Fortunes of Falstaff* (Cambridge, 1944), p. 14.
[4]Bernard Spivack, *Shakespeare and the Allegory of Evil* (Columbia, 1958), p. 170, 386–407.

The limitations of the above theory will be effectively demon-
strated if, leaving out *Richard III* for the moment, we consider
its applicability to *Henry IV* alone. First, even if the Lord Chief
Justice, who is not even named, is taken as a representation of the
rule of law, Hotspur is too subtly drawn to be looked upon as a
mere symbol of anarchic chivalry. What is more damaging to this
moralistic interpretation of *Henry IV* is that it gives a completely
misleading picture of Falstaff. He is indeed a drunkard and a lecher,
but to label him a personification of Vanity is no more adequate
as an explanation of his character than yellow is as a definition of
gold. He is a much more intricate and a much more sympathetic
character than the Sir John Paunch imagined by Quiller-Couch
and Dover Wilson,[1] and that is why the Rejection at the end
produces an impression of discomfort which Shakespeare himself
seems to have anticipated, and tried to counter by holding forth
the assurance which he did not honour that he would continue
the story of the old knight in his account of the reign of Henry V.
Falstaff is a roisterer and a reveller but he is also the exponent of
an attitude to life which is revealed in its different facets in ten
long acts, and of which, in spite of the Rejection at the end of
2 *Henry IV*, we have no reason to think Shakespeare totally
disapproved. When Falstaff ridicules Puritanism by describing
his sins in scriptural phraseology, he does it with so much grace
and with such inverted appropriateness that we feel that here, if
anywhere, we hear the voice of Shakespeare himself, inveighing
against the cramping effect of religion and morals. Even if we
leave Shakespeare the man out of account, he must have been a
poor dramatic moralist if he intended to present such an enchant-
ing parodist of the scriptures as a symbol of the loathsomeness of
irreligion.

An equally serious objection – and one that is admitted by the
sponsors of this theory – is that in this play there are really no
alternatives to choose between, even though a tension between
two opposing forces is of the essence of a morality play. Arguing
along the lines laid down by realistic critics, we may say that
Prince Hal's soliloquy at the end of the first tavern scene (1 *Henry
IV*, I. ii) only follows a theatrical convention of giving information
to the audience. But the speech also reflects character, for it
correctly describes the Prince's attitude throughout the whole

[1] A. Quiller-Couch, *Shakespeare's Workmanship* (Cambridge, 1919), pp. 135 ff. Dover-
Wilson, *The Fortunes of Falstaff*.

course of the story. All through the play he looks upon his boon companions as base contagious clouds that seem to strangle him but cannot. He does not take part in the Gadshill robbery; he only robs the robbers, and in trying to outwit Falstaff is overwhelmed by Falstaff's lying like truth. Although a 'good angel' to Falstaff, he sees that the money robbed is 'paid back again' – a procedure which Falstaff disapproves of as 'double labour'. Indeed, Shakespeare's purpose here seems to be to show that the youthful riotousness alleged by chroniclers against Henry V was only a cloak behind which his greatness lay unbedimmed. It is his father and others who are deceived by appearances; he himself is never the victim of temptation or self-deception. When the call of duty comes he responds to it spontaneously – and without a twinge; he is friends with his father and goes forth to battle, not recklessly like Hotspur, but with courage and a full awareness of the risks involved:

> The land is burning; Percy stands on high;
> And either we or they must lower lie.
>
> (1 *Henry IV*, III. iii. 225–6)

Where is the temptation and where is the choice? Falstaff does, indeed, ask him, now that he is friends with his father, to rob the royal exchequer, but the Prince takes no notice of the suggestion. Nor is he a lecher or a lady-killer, and it is noteworthy that even in the midst of riotous merry-making his dealings with women are impeccable. He is never guilty of any impropriety towards Mistress Quickly and is not even acquainted with Doll Tearsheet. In spite of what the Lord Chief Justice says about separating him from Falstaff, he does return to his low companions and mixes freely with them, but now, too, he maintains his old aloofness. When Poins broaches the subject of his father's illness, his answer is characteristic: 'By this hand, thou thinkest me as far in the devil's book as thou and Falstaff for obduracy and persistency: let the end try the man. But I tell thee my heart bleeds inwardly that my father is so sick; and keeping such vile company as thou art hath in reason taken from me all ostentation of sorrow.' (2 *Henry IV*, II. ii. 50–56).

The only effect vile company has on him is that it has taken away all ostentation of sorrow. Whether his heart bleeds inwardly is another matter, one with which we are not concerned here. This dialogue shows, further, that although a good mixer, he is not for a moment forgetful of the difference in rank and character between himself and the vile company he keeps. When Poins proposes that he and the Prince disguise themselves as drawers, his reaction is characteristic: 'From a god to a bull! a heavy descension! it was Jove's case. From a prince to a prentice! a low transformation! that shall be mine; for in every thing the purpose must weigh with the folly'' (ibid., 192–6.)

His purpose weighs with the folly when it is no more than making a fool of Falstaff, but when weightier matters are before him he casts off his folly without a moment's thought. It is only once that he has occasion to reproach himself for neglect of serious duties; when he is busy eavesdropping on Falstaff in his amours and twitting the old rogue, news comes of a tempest of commotion, and he blames himself for idly profaning his precious time when the country is torn with civil dissension. But the quick and curt farewell he gives to Falstaff – 'Falstaff, good night' – and the alacrity with which he hurries to the post of duty show that he was not 'engraffed to Falstaff', never tempted or deluded as the protagonist of a morality play should be. However painful the final Rejection might be, it was not sudden; neither was it the result of a deliberate choice made at a particular moment, and it was not also due to the intercession of any heavenly power. Even the harried Lord Chief Justice, now exalted to unlooked for honours and authority, is as much taken by surprise as Falstaff. 'I know thee not, old man', says Henry V on ascending the throne, but he never knew the old man in any intimate sense of the term. He kept the rogue's company partly for a brief holiday, and largely for astounding the world by the denouement of the Rejection, when by dismissing the fat knight the lean prig would be able to shine like the sun emerging from the clouds. There is nothing of the morality pattern in this game of the sun and clouds.

III

The theory that Shakespeare's historical plays embody the Tudor view of history has received wide currency and should be examined in some detail. The Tudor myth effectively propagated in the time of Henry VII and encouraged in that of his successors has to be related to the medieval concept of life. Although medieval writers were interested in the progress of mundane affairs and some medieval chroniclers like Froissart had a shrewd sense of history, the medieval outlook on life – if the generaliza-

tion may be permitted – was singularly unhistorical. The mind of
medieval Europe was dominated by theology and the principal
tenet of medieval Catholicism was the omnipresence of God for
whom all things exist simultaneously and in whose knowledge
there can be no discursiveness. 'In our knowledge', says St
Thomas Aquinas, 'there is a double process; one of succession
only, when from actually understanding one object we turn our
attention to another; the other of causality, as when we arrive
at conclusions through principles. The first process cannot apply
to God, for the multiple objects we understand successively when
they are taken in themselves, can be understood all at once when
they are seen in one principle. God sees everything in one, namely,
in himself alone. Nor does the second process apply; first, because
it entails succession, for in working from principles to conclusions,
we do not simultaneously consider them both; secondly, because
it is a process from the known to the unknown'.[1]

The predominant idea in this theological view of life – according
to St Thomas, wisdom is equivalent to theology – is of order and
unity. All life emanates from God who is one, and although there
are contingent occurrences, all mutable things go back to a first
immutable. So long as the Church retained its supremacy and
theology was relied on to govern other sciences and set them in
proportion, history was free to explore contingent occurrences
and to satisfy men's curiosity about past happenings, because there
was the implicit conviction that there was nothing ultimate in
such happenings; and when two sciences – say theology and
history – are engaged, their respective conclusions need not be
taken as counterbalancing each other for the lower should be
subsumed under the higher. 'Man', says St Thomas Aquinas, 'is
directed to his ultimate end by the notion of the first cause, and
to his proximate end by the notion of subordinate movers, as the
soldier is directed to victory by the high command, and to his
tactical dispositions by the regimental commander'.[2] Looked at
from this point of view, all events, even those which seem to be
fortuitous, may be properly orientated, and then comprehended
in the order of divine providence. The Thomist view of the
universe finds adequate expression in Dante's *Divina Commedia*, in
which even capricious Fortune is looked upon as a part of the
divine order:

---

[1] *The Works of St Thomas Aquinas: Philosophical Texts* (ed. Gilby, London, 1956), p. 101.
[2] ibid., p. 66.

> Her permutations never know truce nor pause;
> Necessity lends her speed, so swift in fame
> Men come and go, and cause succeeds to cause.
>
> (Inferno, VII. 88–90, tr. D. Sayers)

Dante does not ascribe the course of history to blind chance; for him in spite of fortuitous happenings the universe is like a book in which accidents are bound up with substances as leaves in one volume.

Other medieval writers had not the same assurance, but when confronted by the topsyturvydom of mundane affairs they too tried to explain it by means of their other-worldly philosophy. Medieval theology was anxious to inculcate the virtue of laying up one's treasures in heaven, and one of the surest methods of this propaganda would be to expatiate on the disaster that was to overtake human aspirations after wordly power or wealth. It was shown that vice was sure to bring its own punishment, and if a moralist failed to connect a person's unhappy ending with any known vice, he would try to invent one. Dido, as Virgil presents her, is a spotless heroine whose misfortune is undeserved. But Lydgate argues that it was wrong of Dido to remain unprovided with lovers, and noble matrons should not imitate her example.[1] There are occasions, however, when even such excuses cannot be found, and the accepted medieval view is that tragedy is only the story of misfortune, of decline from prosperity:

> Tragedie is to seyn a certeyn storie,
> As olde bokes maken us memorie,
> Of him that stood in greet prosperitee
> And is y-fallen out of heigh degree
> Into miserie, and endeth wrecchedly.[2]

It is immaterial whether this fall from prosperity is deserved or undeserved, and Chaucer's Monk, who gives the above definition, does not mention any hamartia. Tragedy, however, represents only one aspect of life. Comedy gives us the other side of it, for it exchanges a sad beginning for a happy ending: *Est autem comœdia poesis, exordium triste, laeto fine commutans.* 'This is', says Nevill Coghill, 'comedy as Dante, Chaucer, and Lydgate knew and understood it'.[3] Vincent de Beauvais, the author of this defini-

---

[1] John Lydgate, *Falls of Princes*, ed. Henry Bergen (Washington, 1923–27), p. 261.
[2] *The Monk's Tale*: The Prologue, 11. 85–89.
[3] *Shakespeare Survey*, Vol. 8, p. 17.

tion, does not say that the happiness at the end is deserved.

What is more relevant is that happiness is not likely to remain permanent. The most popular symbol of medieval times is that of the Wheel of Fortune, which in its ceaseless rotation takes a man as surely from prosperity to adversity as from adversity to prosperity. Following Boccaccio, Lydgate portrays Fortune as a 'double fals goddesse' with a hundred hands, who lifts men to high estate and then casts them down to adversity. She is partly an engine of retribution, punishing princes for such vices as pride and covetousness, but she is essentially changeable and does not require any excuse for plunging them down from 'al ther great richesse'. This is all due to Adam's fall from Paradise, and now man is doomed. Reference may be made to the fate of Arsinoe whose sons were for no fault murdered by Cereaunus or of the Scipios who laboured for the community but died in ignominy.[1] The only way to fight Fortune is to cultivate the virtue of fortitude or Glad Poverty, which defies changes in material conditions and sets its trust wholly in Jesus, who 'may best in myscheeff helpe'.

Tudor historiography had its roots in medieval thought and could not get rid of its medieval heritage, but its outlook was essentially humanist and largely free from the domination of theology. It tried to explain human affairs in a human way, laying emphasis on secondary and contingent causes, and although not denying the first cause, keeping it as far as possible in the background. The activities of the 'stormy queen' Fortune were regarded as caprices of chance, and Sidney, a typical Renaissance critic who found history an incomplete discipline, tried to remedy its defects not by cultivating the spirit of De Contemptu Mundi but by escaping into the golden world delivered by poetry.[2] Secondly, Tudor historians were fervent nationalists, far different in their outlook from the medieval chronicler who saw history from a universal point of view, 'not as a play of mere human purposes, in which he took the side of his friend, but as a process, having an objective necessity of its own'.[3] Although nationalism was not unknown in the Middle Ages, its impact was not felt in medieval historiography. In Tudor historical writing there is, in spite of moralization on the inevitability of retribution and the

---

[1] *Falls of Princes*, pp. 551, 633.
[2] *Apologie for Poetrie* (ed. Churton Collins, Oxford), p. 8, pp. 14–24.
[3] R. G. Collingwood, *The Idea of History* (Oxford Paperbacks, 1961), p. 53.

instability of Fortune in the medieval manner, a noticeable change both in content and attitude. The themes are taken largely from English history and only occasionally from legends; the moralization is generally political and the tone pronouncedly nationalist. Indeed, even where the subject is feudal warfare, there is a recognition of the force of nationalism which ran counter to feudal claims. Tudor historians glorify Henry V, whose title to the French throne would appear to be absurd by modern standards. But Hall admits that the English king was in France 'a straunge Potestat', 'a forein prince', and Henry himself, in the course of one of his orations, said that his enemies, the people of France, formed 'one nacion of one language and one country.'[1] Hall's book was designed as a moral discourse on the evils of civil dissension, and his principal illustration was the loss of French possessions as a result of warring factions in the government of England. Yet both Hall and Polydore Vergil admit that the English were driven out of France largely on account of the readiness of the French – they, of course, call it 'perfidy' – to throw off the foreign yoke.

Another remarkable pointer to the change in outlook – from the theological to the political – is furnished by the *Mirror for Magistrates*, which was intended as a continuation of Boccaccio's *De Casibus Virorum Illustrium* and Lydgate's *Falls of Princes*. The *Mirror* moralizes on vice bringing its own punishment and also on the capriciousness of Fortune, but its moralization is not 'universalistic' as in Boccaccio or Lydgate. Not only are the protagonists all English (or Scottish), but the monologues in which the unfortunate men recount the stories of their life on earth try, however haltingly, to build a working political theory that would help magistrates, who are the king's deputies, in the work of government. The period especially chosen by the authors of this miscellany as well as by some other writers is the stretch of about a hundred years between Richard II and Richard III, and all the calamities which happened between the accession of Henry IV (1399) and that of Henry VII (1485) were traced to the original sin of the deposition and murder of Richard II. Bolingbroke had an unquiet time as king, and if the curse was suspended for some years after his death it was due to the exceptional prowess and piety of his son. But it fell with redoubled force on his grand-

---

[1]Hall's *Chronicle, Containing the History of England during the Reign of Henry the Fourth and the Succeeding Monarchs to the End of the Reign of Henry the Eighth* (London, 1808), p. 85.

son, and an appropriate prophecy as well as an appropriate precedent was found for this delayed retribution. This disingenuous
explanation was no answer to the political-ethical problem which
lay behind the horrors of the Wars of the Roses. If Bolingbroke
were a usurper, it should be no sin to dethrone him or people
lineally descended from him, and in this way the rising of the
Percies on behalf of Mortimer and the subsequent Yorkist intrigues would be the assertion of right against might. But Hall
slurs over the problem and looks upon all rebellion against the
reigning monarch as sinful. Much as he blames Bolingbroke, the
Oxford conspiracy to restore Richard II is for him a mischief set
forth by the Devil, and when the Percies rise in arms against
Henry IV, the King's cause is right and his quarrel just. King-
maker Warwick is a mighty figure in Shakespeare's 2 *Henry VI*
and 3 *Henry VI*, but his attitude to the basic problem is comically
self-contradictory. In the earlier stages of the Wars of the Roses,
he stands up for the 'right' of the Duke of York, but later on he
regrets that for the house of York he 'put Henry from his native
right'.

In the *Mirror*, the Duke of York has no doubt that he has a better
title to the throne than Henry VI, but he is cruelly killed and
humiliated by the Lancastrians. The conclusion he arrives at is
unconnected with the political problem raised by him:

> Wherefore warne princes not to wade in warre,
> For any cause, except the realmes defence:
> Their troublous titles are unwurthy farre,
> The blud, the lyfe, the spoyle of innocence.
>
> (*Richard, Duke of York*, 162–5)

Henry VI, his opposite number, lives 'so cleare a life', and yet
he too had 'cruell lucke'. The moral lesson preached by him is
equally tame; it could have been drawn by any medieval moralist,
for it has nothing specifically Tudor about it. Misfortunes are
caused by divine will which 'appoynteth payne for good mens
exercise' and by sin which 'God doth highly hate' and which
deserves due punishment. The valiant Earl of Salisbury, who was
slain at Orleans, probes the question deeper, but he too fails to
come to a very satisfactory conclusion. His father John, Lord
Montacute, was beheaded by Henry IV for taking part in the
Oxford conspiracy 'to restore Kyng Richard to the rose'. The
cause was right, but

> How many agayn through helpe of fortune blind,
> For yll attemptes atchieved, with honour blest?
> Sucess is wurst ofttimes whan cause is best,
> Therefore say I: God send them sory happes,
> That judge the causes by their after clappes.
>
> (*Thomas, Earl of Salisbury*, 24–28)

But what should the righteous man do? Should he suffer wrongs in silence and allow things to drift from bad to worse? That is the tame ending to the Earl's rigmarole:

> Who furdereth right is not thereby excused,
> If through the same he do sum other wrong:
> To every vice due guerdon doth belong.
>
> (ibid., 75–77)

Tudor political philosophy was indecisive, ambiguous, and confused, because there was a basic contradiction in the Tudor postulate about history and politics. At the time that the Battle of Bosworth Field was fought, there was little doubt that Richard III was established on the throne and he had possibly then the best title to it, certainly a better title than could be claimed by the Earl of Richmond, who had only a distant connexion with the house of Lancaster. But the question cannot be disposed of so simply. The Lancastrian family was in possession when the Duke of York disturbed the existing arrangement, although he had an arguably better case than the Lancastrians. So from the politico-moral point of view the Wars of the Roses seemed to have no end, for here one right was contending against another, and factions were irreconcilable and almost equally balanced. Even when Richard III is firmly entrenched, he cannot trust Buckingham, his 'other self' and 'counsel's consistory', for that deep-revolving Duke is, after all, a Lancastrian.[1] Only Richmond could deliver the people out of the shambles to which England had been reduced, because although not a direct descendant – in *Richard III*, Queen Margaret never mentions him – he is connected with the house of Lancaster, and in his favour Buckingham waives his own claim. And Elizabeth is the indubitable heir of Edward IV. By marrying her Richmond would unite the two Roses and put an end to civil dissension. This was a working arrangement, and it worked well. But it would be unsafe to deduce any political

---

[1] It should be pointed out, however, that Shakespeare never mentions Buckingham as a possible claimant to the throne.

philosophy or moral maxim from such a compromise. It is reasonable to think that Shakespeare, who presents Bolingbroke as a saviour in *Richard II* and as a usurper with a stricken conscience in 2 *Henry IV*, who does not mention the Mortimer claim in *Henry V* but dilates on it in *Henry IV* and *Henry VI*, interpreted history aesthetically rather than philosophically and presented every point of view for its dramatic significance rather than for its doctrinal value. Having stated the central paradox in the Tudor position, we may proceed to a closer examination of the dominant ideas in Tudor historiography and see how Shakespeare presents them in his historical plays.

IV

Such ideas may be reduced to three: (i) English nationalism, (ii) absolute obedience to the reigning monarch, and (iii) order and unity. These ideas have been so powerfully expressed in Shakespeare's historical dramas that many critics think that they were intended by him as political moralities and that it is from that point of view that their dramatic significance ought to be judged. There are minor differences between one writer and another, and there are some critics who think that Shakespeare expressed the opposition point of view rather than the one officially encouraged, but it is generally held that the histories differ from the comedies and tragedies largely because of their politico-ethical emphasis.

If, however, the plays are considered *as* plays, it will appear very doubtful whether Shakespeare was primarily interested in propagating any particular political or moral idea. Rather it will seem that Elizabethan notions of history were part of the raw materials he transformed, and only remotely connected with the ultimate dramatic effect of his plays. Not that Shakespeare was unpatriotic or did not seriously mean what he said so eloquently through John of Gaunt in *Richard II* and the Bastard in *King John;* but although these passionate outbursts have an appeal of their own, it is in the dramatic context that their appropriateness can be properly realized. John of Gaunt's poetical glorification of This other Eden, this demi-paradise, must be seen as a part of his indictment of Richard who is ruining the beautiful land; and it lends support to those who would afterwards save England from the reckless tyrant. The theme of the play is the deposition of an anointed but unworthy king, and this speech has to be set against the Bishop of Carlisle's plea later on that no subject has the right to judge or depose God's deputy on earth. Indeed, immediately after delivering that eloquent oration on the beauty and glory of England, Gaunt says that Richard's actions are tantamount to suicide – 'Thou diest' – and then points out that although he may be God's anointed, he deserves to be deposed:

> O! had thy grandsire, with a prophet's eye,
> Seen how his son's son should destroy his sons,
> From forth thy reach he would have laid thy shame,
> Deposing thee before thou were possess'd,
> Which art possess'd now to depose thyself.
> (Richard II, II. i. 104–08)

It is the tension between these two ideas – the necessity or desirability of deposing a bad king and the inviolability of his position and person – that is one of the strands of the complex web of this drama.

As king, John was possibly worse than Richard II. Richard's alleged murder of his uncle is only reported and not represented on the stage, but the atrocity which was intended against Arthur is a part of the action of King John. Moreover, John – in Shakespeare's drama – is admittedly a usurper, occupying the throne more by strong possession than by rightful title. It may be that Shakespeare deliberately chose this subject as suitable for the inculcation of militant nationalism, because he would be able to show that the country is greater than the King. Behind John looms the mighty figure of the Bastard, who professes to follow Commodity but really stands for national unity and unflinching loyalty to the country:

> Now these her princes are come home again,
> Come the three corners of the world in arms,
> And we shall shock them. Naught shall make us rue,
> If England to itself do rest but true.
> (King John, V. vii. 115–18)

Although patriotism or united resistance to a foreign invader may be looked upon as the leit motif of King John, it is an idea that emerges living and vibrant and not a moral lesson that is expounded. For if the argument is carried to its logical conclusion, the play might be interpreted, as indeed it has been, as a satire on kingship, and then its ideological significance runs counter to a favourite Tudor doctrine – the unquestionable supremacy of the king. Tudor history would never tolerate the separation of king and country, and Shakespeare, unlike Bale, refuses to make a hero of John, while he also omits the long didactic speeches in which the author of *The Troublesome Raigne* inculcates endurance of tyranny. It would be absurd, therefore, to claim that Shakespeare was preaching English nationalism independently of English 'royalism', though that is the idea which emanates from the play.

If Shakespeare's historical plays are interpreted as political moralities, there would be confusion and contradiction at every step. *Henry V*, for example, would present a thesis that would clash with the lesson conveyed in *King John*. Henry V lays claim to the throne of France through a woman, and that is exactly the French Dauphin's title to the throne of England. Lewis, as Holinshed tells us, 'defended the cause that moved him to take upon him this journey into England, disproving not onelie the right which King John had to the crowne, but also alledging his owne interest, not onelie by his new election of the barons, but also in the title of his wife, whose mother the queene of Castile remained onelie alive of all brethren and sisters of Henrie the second late King of England'.[1] It is not reasonable to suppose that Shakespeare would be blind to the implications of his own theme. If preaching nationalism had been his dominant purpose, would he have written two such plays as *King John* and *Henry V*, inspiring national resistance against a foreign foe in one of them and inciting foreign aggression in the other? In an earlier play – 1 *Henry VI* – the patriotic note, strangely enough, is struck not so much by the English lords, who for all their prowess look like free-booters in a country not their own, but by England's enemies – the Pucelle and the Duke of Burgundy. Joan looks upon herself as a person divinely assigned to be the English scourge in order to free her country from alien domination, and she is the only person in the whole trilogy to speak of 'country' and 'countrymen'. Although she makes a cruel comment on Burgundy's turning and turning again as only a Frenchman may be expected to do, even this joke stems from a passionate love of her country, and she converts the slippery Duke by a fervent appeal to his patriotic sentiments:

---

[1] R. Holinshed, *Chronicles of England, Scotland, and Ireland* (London, 1807–08), p. 330.

Behold the wounds, the most unnatural wounds,
Which thou thyself hast giv'n her woeful breast.
O! turn thy edged sword another way;
Strike those that hurt, and hurt not those that help.
One drop of blood drawn from thy country's bosom,
Should grieve thee more than streams of foreign gore:
Return thee therefore, with a flood of tears,
And wash away thy country's stained spots.

(1 *Henry VI*, III. iii. 50–57)

If Shakespeare meant England to be the protagonist of his historical plays, he would not have made Joan of Arc, who was 'devil or devil's dam' to the English, the mouthpiece of patriotic resistance to foreign aggression; and he would not have extolled in *Henry V* what he cries down in *King John*. Although to an Elizabethan Chauvinist – let us imagine that Shakespeare wanted to represent such sentiment – English aggression on France would be different from a French invasion of England, as a moralist Shakespeare must have realized that the difference between the two was as between tweedledum and tweedledee. And there is the further consideration that although Shakespeare boosts Henry V's victories and seems to present him as an epic hero, he also makes the Chorus warn the audience at the end of the play that the English success is only a temporary adventure and that all that Henry has gained will be lost by his son.

Shakespeare's treatment of the second dominant idea in Tudor historical writing – that of absolute royal supremacy – has already been touched on above; here, too, the crucial play is *Richard II*, where a king is deposed by a usurper who unleashes the forces of retribution that are stayed during his son's reign but devastate England in the third generation. When Bolingbroke ascends the throne, the Bishop of Carlisle sounds a stern note of warning:

My Lord of Hereford here, whom you call king,
Is a foul traitor to proud Hereford's king;
And if you crown him, let me prophesy,
The blood of English shall manure the ground
And future ages groan for this foul act;
Peace shall go sleep with Turks and infidels,
And in this seat of peace tumultuous wars
Shall kin with kin and kind with kind confound;
Disorder, horror, fear and mutiny

Shall here inhabit, and this land be call'd
The field of Golgotha and dead men's skulls.

(*Richard II*, IV. i. 134–44)

Not only does he prove a true prophet, but even in his own lifetime, the usurper acknowledges the honourableness of his conduct
and, indirectly, the justness of his argument. When exiling him,
Bolingbroke says:

So, as thou livest in peace, die free from strife:
For though mine enemy thou hast ever been,
High sparks of honour in thee have I seen.

(ibid., V. vi 27–9)

Richard himself thinks that he is God's anointed, and therefore
inviolable. Shakespeare draws such a vivid picture of the reluctant
pangs of abdicating Royalty that we are tempted to think that he
himself regarded the deposition as a sacrilege. But even in
Shakespeare's lifetime the followers of the Earl of Essex staged
this play on the eve of the Earl's rebellion, and Queen Elizabeth
herself said that she was likened to the deposed King.[1] The
sponsors of the rebellion would not have staged *Richard II* if they
thought that it condemned the seizure of the crown by Bolingbroke. Indeed, in Shakespeare's play – if not exactly in the
chronicles – Richard surrenders the crown more than Bolingbroke snatches it from him. If in the base court (III. iii), when
Bolingbroke said, in terms of his promise, 'My gracious lord, I
come but for mine own,' Richard had taken him at his word, and
following Aumerle's advice, had fought with gentle words till
Time lent friends and friends their swords, one cannot say whether
Bolingbroke would have seized the throne or not. But instead of
doing so Richard says that he is Bolingbroke's and all, calls the
latter his heir, and proceeds to surrender the crown which even
then he might have tried to retain. No one in *Richard II* accuses
Bolingbrooke of being false to his oath. The indictment on the
usurpation is uttered by Bolingbroke's enemies – the Bishop of
Carlisle in *Richard II*, and Hotspur and Worcester in 1 *Henry IV*,
and alone of these men Worcester – rather late in the day –
accuses the King of having forgotten the oath made to them at
Doncaster (V. i. 58). Shakespeare observes the same neutrality

---

[1]Although all critics do not agree that this was the play staged by Shakespeare's company
on the day before the Essex rising, the balance of evidence is in favour of such a supposition.
(See *PMLA*, Vol. XLII, pp. 686–720; Vol. XLVI, pp. 694–719).

of tone with regard to the rebellion of the Percies. He holds no brief for the conspirators; Hotspur, for all his greatness, is a madcap, Worcester a malevolent and perfidious intriguer, Northumberland a backslider, Mortimer a nincompoop, and Glendower a braggart and a fool. But although victory comes deservedly to the King and his son, the arguments advanced by the conspirators remain unanswered, and the final act of perjury which puts an end to the rebellion only shows how ungodly God's deputies may be.

The third leading idea of Tudor historiography – love for order and hatred of dissension – is repeatedly and strongly expressed in some of the plays, but once again it will be wrong to hold that the significance of any of them centres on this idea. *King John* ends with a passionate appeal to Englishmen to close their ranks in face of foreign aggression. The opening scene of 1 *Henry VI* is conceived in the spirit of Hall, who wrote his history to show 'What mischiefe hath insurged in realmes by intestine devision, what depopulacion hath ensued in countries by civill discension, what detestable murder hath been committed in citees by separate faccions, and what calamities hath ensued in famous regions by domesticall discords and unnaturall controversy'.[1] The defeat of Talbot, later on in the play, is represented as due mostly to the rivalry of York and Somerset; the destruction caused by internecine strife during the Wars of the Roses is luridly described; and the advent of Henry VII, who unites the two Roses, is shown as providential. But this moral lesson about unity and order, although it acquires prominence towards the end of *King John*, occurs intermittently in the three parts of *Henry VI*, and is also enforced at the conclusion of *Richard III*, is no part of the substance of these dramas, and the other 'histories' have very little to do with it. In *King John*, the English lords do unite after Melun's disclosures, but the Dauphin is persuaded to sue for peace as much by this new alignment of forces as by the sinking of his supply ships and his ignorance of a similar disaster to the Bastard's army. Nor should we attach much importance – dramatically – to the political significance of the Earl of Richmond's victory in the last act of *Richard III*. It is like the conventional ending in Bernard Shaw's unconventional plays. Such a conclusion flattered Tudor political sentiment and, what is more important, it draws the long tetralogy – a story of violence and unnatural strife – to a

---

[1] Hall's *Chronicle*, p. 1.

peaceful end. There is no reason to believe that such a conclusion is an integral part of the tetralogy, or even of *Richard III*, which is a tragedy of Richard's downfall and not a comedy of Richmond's triumph. Richmond appears once in 3 *Henry VI* merely to give King Henry an opportunity for making a prophecy. This episode, although drawn from history, is irrelevant to the dramatic context, and Richmond appears only in the last act of *Richard III*, where he just defeats Richard and wrests the crown from him. If it had been Shakespeare's intention to give primacy to the moral lesson to be derived from Richmond's triumph and his oration on unity and order, he would certainly have given him a more important place in the main body of the play. That would have made it more effective as a morality but possibly weakened it as a drama.

The evil effects of civil strife are, indeed, forcefully presented in 1 *Henry VI* and also in 3 *Henry VI*, II. v, where a Father has killed his Son and a Son his Father, and there are other references to this theme scattered in different parts of the trilogy. It will, however, be doing injustice to the multiple interest of these plays if this theme is given more prominence than others. Rather *Henry VI* is dramatically effective more because of the clash of rival personalities – Talbot against Joan, Gloucester against Winchester and Suffolk, York against Somerset and Margaret – than on account of the civil dissensions which throw these personal clashes into relief. But for the warring factions and the general turmoil, Richard, Earl of Warwick or Richard, Duke of Gloucester would not have come into prominence, but it is these and other flamboyant personalities who dominate the trilogy and give it its dramatic interest. Even in the episodes which are directly connected with the theme of civil faction, Shakespeare transcends the purely didactic significance of the incidents in order to bring out their dramatic appeal. Henry VI's marriage to Margaret helps to sharpen the animosities of the barons, but Shakespeare lays emphasis on the romance of Suffolk's wooing, the arrogance of the Duchess of Gloucester and the rivalry between her and the new Queen – episodes which are largely un-historical and only remotely political. Although Jack Cade's rebellion, which was engineered by the Duke of York, is a direct offshoot of the Wars of the Roses, the dramatic interest of the episode is nevertheless derived, as will be seen in greater detail later on, from the character of Jack Cade and not from the political implications of his misdeeds. Jack Cade disturbs order in civil

THE SUBSTANCE OF SHAKESPEARE'S 'HISTORIES'   25

society and Alexander Iden restores it by killing Cade. Iden
delivers an elaborate sermon on the philosophy of order which
Shakespeare is supposed to have embodied in his historical plays:

> Lord! who would live turmoiled in the court,
> And may enjoy such quiet walks as these?
> This small inheritance my father left me
> Contenteth me, and worth a monarchy.
> I seek not to wax great by others' waning,
> Or gather wealth I care not with what envy:
> Sufficeth that I have maintains my state,
> And sends the poor well pleased from my gate.
>
> (2 Henry VI, IV. x. 18–25)

This should be contrasted with Jack Cade's vision of violent
disorder in the state:

> There shall be in England seven halfpenny loaves sold for a penny;
> the three-hooped pot shall have ten hoops; and I will make it felony to
> drink small beer. All the realm shall be in common, and in Cheapside
> shall my palfry go to grass.
>
> (ibid., IV. ii, 73–78)

Irving Ribner places these two passages side by side in order to
bring out the political lesson implied by their contrast,[1] but he
does not notice that the first passage, although written in verse,
is prosaic and dull, but the second is dramatically vivid. Many
readers would fail to recall Iden, but who can forget Jack Cade?
Unlike his son, Henry V was a very powerful king who had no
reason to be afraid of civil disorder. He would not scruple to
'awake (his) sleeping sword of war' if political necessity or a just
title demanded it. For him mere order is stagnation, a part of idle
Ceremony:

> O ceremony, show me but thy worth:
> What is thy soul of adoration?
> Art thou aught else but place, degree, and form,
> Creating awe and fear in other men?
>
> (Henry V, IV. i. 264–7)

Ulysses, in Troilus and Cressida, praises 'degree' only to explain
the temporary eclipse of the Greek army in Troy and to wean
away Achilles from indolent retirement. But Henry V, arrayed
like Mars, disturbs 'place, degree, and form', because he knows

---

[1] The English History Play in the Age of Shakespeare (Princeton, 1957), pp. 107–08.

that he can restore order, and impose his will even in a foreign country. Emphasis is laid in the three parts of *Henry VI* on the necessity for unity, and in the later portions of the trilogy there is expressed a longing for peace and order, but that is because the country has been ravaged by civil strife. There is faction in *Henry VIII*, too, where the barons and the prelates are eager to rush at one another's throats. Mighty Buckingham is thought to to be guilty of treason as was the Duke of York, Wolsey is as ambitious of power as King-maker Warwick, soft-hearted Katharine is as much opposed to Wolsey as Margaret, She-wolf of France, was to Humphrey, and Cranmer is drawn into a net by the Lord Chancellor and Bishop Gardiner as Humphrey was by Suffolk and Cardinal Beaufort. But in this play there is no moralizing on 'degree' or order or on the evils of dissension, because when the necessity arises the King is powerful enough to set everybody in his proper place.

The idea that Shakespeare in his historical plays tried to express the Tudor view of history is somewhat 'naïve', and some critics not without justification have gone to the opposite extreme of suggesting 'that there was a political current in Shakespeare's mind, which in the days of Elizabeth led him into opposition'.[1] On this view, Shakespeare was obliged to use words which might be plausibly explained, but under a veneer of conformity he concealed scathing criticism of the established order. As pointed out already, Henry V makes out an elaborate plea about the justness of his title to the French throne but Queen Elinor depends more on strong possession than on right. In *Richard II*, 'the depreciation of the people and the exaggeration of the royal prerogative are put into the mouths of favourites and evil counsellors'. If *Henry IV*, *Henry V*, and *Henry VI* are viewed as a single dramatic unit, it will be seen that 'the constant prominence of the law which fatally conducts traitors to punishment is . . . modified by a large-hearted sympathy with their grievances and temptations'.[2] In fact, Shakespeare has no definite answer to give to the problems of political right or political justice, nor does he seem to be interested in them. He shows that Henry IV might be a usurper but Richard II did not deserve to rule. He never suggests a clear answer to the basic questions which lay behind the carnage of the Wars of the Roses: Who had the better right to the throne – Henry VI or the

---

[1] R. Simpson, *The Politics of Shakespeare's Historical Plays* (Sh. Soc. Trans., 1874), p. 440.
[2] ibid., p. 409, 415.

Duke of York? Does Henry VI suffer for his grandfather's sin? Or does he deserve to be cashiered on account of his own incompetence? And do not these two concepts contradict each other? 'In *Henry VI*', says Brockbank, 'the sacrificial idea, which makes catastrophe a consequence of sin is sharply challenged by the "machiavellian" idea that makes it a consequence of weakness'.[1] Those who believe that Shakespeare was primarily interested in dramatizing the political assumptions of Tudor monarchy think that he gave in his political plays his concept of the ideal king, the type of sovereign that should succeed Elizabeth. 'The central and continuous image in these plays, more specific than a mood, more comprehensive than a character, is, I believe', says Ellis-Fermor, 'a composite figure – that of the statesman-king, the leader and public man, which Shakespeare builds up gradually through the series of political plays from *Henry VI* to *Henry V*'.[2] But other critics have found in these plays a point of view or a bias of an opposite character. For Walter Pater the ruling conception under which Shakespeare arranged the lights and shadows of the story of the English kings is the 'irony of kingship – average human nature, flung with a wonderfully pathetic effect into the vortex of great events'.[3] John Bailey goes a step further and says that though Shakespeare's histories are more royal than national, more personal than political, that is a long way from being all they are. No republican can demand a better text for a sermon against personal monarchy than he can find in scene after scene of Shakespeare's 'histories'.[4]

The historical plays are neither moral homilies nor political treatises. Shakespeare borrowed his incidents from the chronicles and other sources and he sometimes re-told them with little change. But it would be rash to conclude that he merely gave a verse-paraphrase of what he found in his source-books. The changes he made – both in general concept and in details – and even the slight shifts in emphasis when he did not make any large modifications show that he transformed his sources rather than reproduced them. Yet in spite of modifications and shifts of emphasis, these plays are not 'mythical', and the Duke of Marlborough had some justification for saying that he was content to

[1]*Early Shakespeare* (Stratford-on-Avon Studies 3, 1961), p. 83.
[2]Una Ellis-Fermor, *The Frontiers of Drama* (London, 1948), p. 21.
[3]*Appreciations* (Pocket Edition, Calcutta, 1944), p. 181.
[4]John Bailey, *The Continuity of Letters* (Oxford, 1923), p. 62.

know no more English history than what he found in Shakespeare. The difference between history and drama is pithily expressed by Aristotle when he says that dramatic imitators have to represent a story as though they were actually doing the things described.[1] That is to say, the dramatic poet is to identify himself with his characters and to show them as actually doing what history merely reports them as doing. Dramatic poetry has also to follow, like all other forms of art, the law of harmony, and the crowd of incidents and characters must round themselves off into what Carlyle calls 'a kind of rhythmic coherence'.[2] It is for these reasons that the dramatist has to telescope time and space, and not only shorten the sprawling historical narrative but also occasionally add to it.

The causes of action, Aristotle points out, are two: Character, which makes us ascribe certain moral qualities to the agents, and thought, which is shown in the arguments advanced by them in support of a particular point or a general truth. But these two causes run into each other, for our intellectual arguments are coloured by our moral qualities and the intellect influences moral proclivities. Northumberland's advocacy of Bolingbroke's plea and the Bishop of Carlisle's denunciation of it emanate from their characters and their characters are partly moulded by their ways of thought. What it is necessary to emphasize here is that neither set of arguments – Northumberland in *Richard II* acts more than he argues and Carlisle argues more than he acts – is Shakespeare's; he only represents the men as though they were doing the things which historians report they did. In *King John*, the Bastard is shocked at the sight of Arthur's dead body, but he passes over the affair and proceeds to unite England against the aggressor without caring to find out how Arthur met his death; he is too shrewd not to have understood who was at the root of it. In *Richard III*, however, the murder of the Princes in the Tower is the climax to a long series of crimes; as soon as the suggestion is made Buckingham deserts Richard, and after this murder everything goes wrong for the murderer. Are we to conclude that Shakespeare connives at a murder by a reigning sovereign in *King John* and condemns it in *Richard III*? It is in such contradictions that we shall be landed if we pursue political and ethical interpretation to the logical end. Shakespeare, in fact, took all sorts of ideas and

---

[1] *On the Art of Poetry* (tr. Bywater, Oxford, 1948), p. 27.
[2] *Heroes and Hero-Worship*: The Hero as Poet.

arguments, political and moral, and he appropriated for his own use images and expressions he found ready to hand just as he lifted his stories from Hall, Holinshed and other sources. But he transmuted them all; it would, therefore, be equally wrong to emphasize either his medieval heritage of the morality tradition or his political background of Tudor monarchy. He was not a writer of homilies or of political history, though his vision of life included both history and politics.

A dramatist is a creative artist, and not a mere medium like a platinum wire, and he surveys life from a point of view. This means that the poet, too, has his ideas, and since these ideas are aesthetic they are different from the political or moral ideas of his time or of the characters in his work. This ideology, which is an emanation from his plot and characters, is subtler than anything expressed by any one amongst the *dramatis personae*, but it compre-hends all that is said by them. The ideas projected by Shakespeare's 'histories' may be said to be moral, but only in the sense that all thinking about life, or all application of ideas to life, is moral. But the principal characteristic of such ideology is that it cannot be detached from the life portrayed in the dramas, from the move-ment of plot and evolution of character.

CHAPTER TWO

Nature and Fortune

I

ON POLITICAL and moral questions Shakespeare seems to have taken no sides, and that is why many critics look upon him as the ideal poet described by Keats, one who has only a negative capability, who 'is capable of being in uncertainties, mysteries, doubts, without any irritable reaching after fact and reason', or a definite conclusion.[1] Hardin Craig traces Shakespeare's much talked of 'indifference' to a characteristic of the Elizabethan mind, which 'suspends truth, not between hypothesis and verification, but between the affirmative and the negative in debate. . . . It follows also that every question has two sides, and . . . Shakespeare, the acutest of Renaissance thinkers, has a boasted breadth of mind, an ability to see both sides of a question, and a sympathy with all sorts and conditions of men. . . . No one can tell whether Bolingbroke or Richard II is in the right'.[2]

Not that Shakespeare merely 'turns men's actions into poetry' or that his 'histories' are 'rather so many chronicles of kings', in which the business of thirty or forty years is 'cramped into a representation of two hours and a half; which is not to imitate or paint nature, but rather to draw her in miniature, to take her in little'.[3] Shakespeare posits different attitudes, and it is to the uncertainties or ambivalences which result from their juxtaposition that some critics have traced the significance of the historical plays. A. P. Rossiter, who calls these ambivalences the Dialectic of the Histories, points out that to say that Shakespeare dramatized the 'naïve' theory of history propounded by Hall would be to narrow down the significance of these plays: 'There is more in the

---

[1] *Letters* (ed. Buxton Forman, Oxford, 1933), p. 72. Keats himself had Shakespeare in mind when he coined the phrase.

[2] Hardin Craig, *The Enchanted Glass* (Blackwell, 1950), p. 157.

[3] Dryden: *An Essay of Dramatic Poesie* (ed. Nichol Smith, Blackie), p. 31.

dark glass than the moral history of the Lancastrian House of Jeroboam and the happy ending in the dawn of Tudarchy'. Further, to reduce Falstaff to 'little more than a mere symbol of all the fat and idle temptations which royalty rejects' would be to over-simplify one of Shakespeare's subtlest and greatest characters.[1] Rossiter thinks that the significance of the historical plays lies in a sort of ambivalence: 'that two opposed value-judgements are subsumed, and that both are valid'. What is serious is also farcical, and what is pathetic is also absurd. Shakespeare, on this view, accepted the frame of the medieval morality or the Tudor system of Order but he undermined both with subtle equivocations and sly ambiguities. The splendour of the historical pageant is qualified with realistic comedy and behind the comical looms the shadow of 'Obscure tragedy'.[2]

The New Criticism, which derives its inspiration from Coleridge's theory about the reconciliation of opposites, is almost always subtle, sometimes profound, but not infrequently it brings together resemblances and analogies that are far-fetched. To take one example, the Gadshill robbery for Rossiter is 'not mere farce': 'If we "realize" it, in an Usurper's state where Henry's right is only that of might, might only – then what are the Percies and Bolingbrokes but Gadshills, Bardolphs, Petos in Bigger Business?'[3] There is nothing wrong with the argument, but do we notice this doubleness in the play unless we are endowed with a special power of 'realization'? A more serious objection to the theory of ambivalence is that in Shakespeare doubleness or ambiguity is never an end in itself. It always points to a larger vision lying beyond the opposed views presented on the foreground. The significance of As You Like It, for example, lies not in any ambivalence between different theories but in their reaching forward to an all-inclusive philosophy of life. Troilus and Cressida is another play in which different views of life are contrasted, but the contrast points to something beyond ambivalence, to the impossibility of reducing the complexity and subtlety of life to a formula. In the 'histories', too, although different views are presented, Shakespeare delves beneath the doubleness of opposed value-judgements to a core of meaning which is revealed through this opposition but is not identical with it.

---

[1] A. P. Rossiter, *Angel with Horns* (London, 1961), pp. 44–45.
[2] ibid., p. 51, 63.
[3] ibid., p. 53.

II

As Shakespeare's historical dramas deal largely with the falls of princes, we are reminded of such medieval writers as Boccaccio and Lydgate, who emphasized the mutability of Fortune, reminded princes that.

> In worldly worshepe may be no surete,

and asked them to take shelter in Glad Poverty, which the caprices of Fortune would not be able to touch. But by Shakespeare's time this ideal had lost its appeal. The Renaissance was a complex movement with many facets and phases, but its most important characteristic was an upsurge of faith in man, in his dignity and worth as an individual. Shakespeare, the greatest poet of the Renaissance, portrays the ideal of Glad Poverty in the person of Henry VI, who wants to conquer Fortune's spite by living low, where Fortune cannot molest him; but Henry VI is an unheroic, unkingly king who excites as much contempt as sympathy. Nor has Shakespeare much admiration for the merely successful man whom Fortune blesses with both hands full. Such a man is Octavius Caesar about whom Cleopatra, at the nadir of her misfortune, makes the contemptuous comment:

> 'Tis paltry to be Caesar.
> Not being Fortune, he's but Fortune's knave,
> A minister of her will;
> > (*Antony and Cleopatra*, V. ii. 2–4)

In Shakespearian drama even a tender and delicate girl like Desdemona is proud of her downright violence and storm of fortunes. In Renaissance time, the Roman goddess Fortuna was equated with Occasio and acquired the latter's forelock, which had to be firmly grasped if she was not to slip away. Shakespeare does not use this image, but he expresses the idea in a different form through Brutus, one of his tragic heroes:

> There is a tide in the affairs of men,
> Which, taken at the flood, leads on to fortune;
> Omitted, all the voyage of their life
> Is bound in shallows and in miseries.
> > (*Julius Caesar*, IV. iii. 217–20)

Fortune must be taken at the flood or we are lost. Earlier in this play Cassius tried to move Brutus with the assurance:

Men at some time are masters of their fates:
The fault, dear Brutus, is not in our stars,
But in ourselves, that we are underlings.
                                    (ibid., I. ii. 138–40)

At some time. When? That is the question. In the comedies the problem is relatively simple. Falstaff flatters Mistress Ford by drawing a picture of what she might be by virtue of her Nature if Fortune, her foe, were not. In the world of Shakespearian comedy, the enmity of Fortune is conquered by Nature or by Nature's art; indeed Fortune sometimes seems to forget her capriciousness in order to further man's happiness. Constance in *King John* claims that Fortune and Nature joined hands to make her son great and complains that later on Fortune was corrupted, and won from him. But that does not happen in the comedies; here Fortune is subdued to Nature. Helena, for example, has unflinching faith in her natural powers and knows that

> Our remedies oft in ourselves do lie
> Which we ascribe to heaven: the fated sky
> Gives us free scope; only doth backward pull
> Our slow designs when we ourselves are dull.
> What power is it which mounts my loves so high;
> That makes me see, and cannot feed mine eye?
> The mightiest space in fortune nature brings
> To join like likes, and kiss like native things.
>   (*All's Well That Ends Well*, I. i. 235–42)

This is the spirit of Shakespearian comedy – this power of Nature to adjust itself to and conquer Fortune, to take the tide at the flood. Prospero bestirs himself at a particular moment, because he knows that if he does not court the influence of a most auspicious star when it is in the ascendant his fortunes will ever after droop. Whether it is intelligence as in Portia, or a capacity for guessing as in Bassanio, or tactful patience as in Viola, or strong will power as in Petruchio, it is some natural force that conquers Fortune when Fortune seems to be recalcitrant. In *As You Like It*, one of the principal modifications Shakespeare makes in the source story of *Rosalynde* is to give a new concept of the relationship between Fortune and Nature. Lodge makes much of Fortune's capriciousness but in Shakespeare's play Fortune's hostility is subdued by man's character, which is one of 'the lineaments of Nature'. In the forest of Arden, Duke Senior

> Finds tongues in trees, books in the running brooks,
> Sermons in stones, and good in everything.
>
> (II. i. 16–7)

And Amiens congratulates him, saying,

> Happy is your Grace,
> That can translate the stubbornness of fortune
> Into so quiet and so sweet a style.
>
> (ibid., 18–20)

Sometimes it is sheer folly that outwits malevolent Fortune. In *Much Ado About Nothing*, there is the most wonderful example of how Nature's natural may triumph over Fortune, for it is Dogberry, whose deepest yearning is to be written down an ass, who saves Hero when human wisdom flounders.

In Shakespeare's tragedies the picture is different. Nature's livery is so inextricably mixed with fortune's star that one does not know which is which. The cleverest of men may make a goddess of Nature and trust her to conquer Fortune and yet all his plans may turn awry. Malevolent Fortune makes Desdemona drop her handkerchief at the wrong moment, but the critical moment itself is created by the nature of Othello and Iago, and later on the characters of Desdemona and Emilia play their appropriate roles in the pattern woven by Destiny. Fortune is, indeed, a beautiful, blind woman in her gifts, because she showers all that a man could desire on the Prince of Denmark and then places him in a situation in which all his wonderful powers only help to spell disaster. The way in which Nature and Fortune coalesce in these plays cannot be expressed by means of the simple formula: Character is Destiny. Nor can we explain the mystery of human tragedy by shifting the responsibility to an Aristotelian hamartia which seems to live parasitically on a person not generally wicked. Macbeth's criminal ambition enters into the magnificence of his nature and all his qualities and defects have a dynamic role to play in the misplacements ordered by Fortune, who weds him to the wrong woman, makes him meet the Witches at the wrong hour, and sends Duncan to his house on the wrong night.

In *Coriolanus*, an inferior tragedy, Nature and Fortune seem to lie apart. Volumnia suggests that her son should dissemble with his nature where his fortunes and his friends required that he should do so in honour (III. ii. 62), but Menenius knows that his nature is too noble for this wordly game, and the First Patrician says that he has already marred his fortune (III. i. 255). In the historical plays, though in this genre it may not be a mark of inferiority, there is the same lack of coalescence between Fortune and Nature, each of which acquires ascendancy in a haphazard manner. Giddy Fortune is for ever spinning her furious wheel and men and women are rising, ruling, falling and being cast off. It is not a question of personal efficiency or inadequacy. The world of the Histories is larger than that of the Comedies or the Tragedies; for it is not the fates of individuals but of communities and of nations that are involved. Shakespeare's vision is aesthetic rather than ethical. There are occasional anticipations of this amoral, un-medieval attitude in earlier Tudor literature, such as in the story of Collingbourne in the *Mirror for Magistrates:*

> We knowe say they the course of Fortunes wheele,
> How constantly it whyrleth styll about,
> Arrearing nowe, whyle elder headlong reele,
> Howe al the riders alwaye hange in doubt.
> But what for that? We count him but a lowte
> That stickes to mount, and basely like a beast
> Lyves temperately for feare of blockam feast.
>
> (ll. 22–28)

Here the ideal is to mount Fortune's wheel, not to take shelter behind Glad Poverty. The historians are much more homiletic than Shakespeare, who even when he is didactic makes dramatic use of the moral lesson presented. In the sources, Henry VI is said to suffer for his grandfather's sins, but in Shakespeare's plays such moral deductions are made either by Bolingbroke's enemies or by the weakling Henry VI who excuses his own frailty with the plea that his title is weak and moralizes – although in another context – 'That things ill got had ever bad success'.

It is natural also that the Usurper, when seized with disease and old age, should himself have some qualms of conscience about a bold and questionable deed he performed in the past. And it is dramatically appropriate that on the eve of the Battle of Agincourt, Henry V should be troubled by his father's sin, to which, by the way, he owes his own 'rightful' title to the thrones of England and France. But he never mentions it again, and his expiation also is characteristically halting. Not that Shakespeare wanted to exalt Bolingbroke or other people who violated the moral law. It is just that we should never lose sight of the aesthetic significance of his work or give too much prominence to the moral interpretation emphasized in his sources. Both Hall and Polydore Vergil suggest that Queen Margaret's misfortunes were the result of her complicity in the murder of the Duke of Gloucester. But Shakespeare does not point any such moral. More than one chronicler says that the murder of the young Princes in the Tower carried out at the instigation of Richard III was the nemesis of Edward IV's perjury, because when in the course of the Wars of the Roses he returned from his sojourn on the continent he claimed nothing more than his Yorkist possessions, and then went back on his promise. It is characteristic of Shakespeare that he omits all reference to Edward IV's perjury when he represents this gruesome incident in *Richard III*. Even Queen Margaret, who here plays the role of a chorus, never draws any moral lesson. Others tried to mount the Wheel of Fortune by dislodging her, and she only contemplates with sardonic glee the spectacle of their downfall.

III

It is necessary to give a more positive account of this amoral vision of history. Time spins fast, and Fortune's wheel revolves ceaselessly, creating opportunities for some and spelling ruin for others. Man in his pride mounts the wheel, and is also cast off. But even this will be a wrong conclusion, for he hands the torch of life to a more vigorous generation. The most predominant impression produced by Shakespeare's historical plays is of continuity in the flow of life. Bolingbroke replaces Richard II as later Richmond supplants Richard III. Although the men and women are different, and the situations vary in details, the pattern is the same. The lords who make political history being very much alike, it does not matter if Shakespeare mistakes one Mortimer for another, or confuses the first Duke of Somerset with the second or the third Duke with the fourth, or even if he mixes up Richard Nevil with Richard Beauchamp, who were both Earls of Warwick. The kings and the barons are, most of them, valiant fighters who know that right is on the side of might, who are passionately loyal but who can change sides at the first provocation or temptation. All of them try to seize Fortune by the forelock and are generally too engrossed in their adventures to moralize, but when they do draw any moral lesson their attitude is almost always dramatically appropriate. Warwick was a princely baron for whom climbing to the crest of power and being dislodged from there are a part of the day's game. So when he lays down his life, he comments soberly and in a general way on the futility of worldly power and wealth:

> My parks, my walks, my manors that I had,
> Even now forsake me; and, of all my lands
> Is nothing left me but my body's length.
> Why, what is pomp, rule, reign, but earth and dust?
> And, live how we can, yet die we must.
>
> (3 *Henry VI*, V. ii. 24–28)

Reputed to be a butcher's son from Ipswich, Cardinal Wolsey was of lower middle class stock, but in the England of Henry VIII he came to occupy a position as towering as that of Warwick in the Wars of the Roses. His rise was more meteoric, and his fall more spectacular than Warwick's, and the way he bids farewell to his greatness is characteristically magniloquent:

> This is the state of man: to-day he puts forth
> The tender leaves of hopes; to-morrow blossoms,
> And bears his blushing honours thick upon him;
> The third day comes a frost, a killing frost;
> And, when he thinks, good easy man, full surely
> His greatness is a-ripening, nips his root,
> And then he falls, as I do.
>
> (*Henry VIII*, III. ii. 353–9)

Part of the difference between the two passages is due to a general change in Shakespeare's style. But there is no doubt that the moralizing is in both places dramatically appropriate.

Amongst the kings portrayed by Shakespeare, there were two weaklings – Richard II and Henry VI; Richard II had nothing to support him except 'some few vanities', and Henry VI little but his holiness. No wonder that these two kings love to moralize on events which they are powerless to control. Henry VI wistfully enlarges on a life of Glad Poverty, and Richard II, equally characteristically, lingers lovingly on the griefs he has got in exchange for his kingdom. The majority of kings and barons in Shakespeare's 'histories' are sturdy adventurers, who challenge Fortune and try to wrest power and glory from the clouds. Their attitude is expressed by Edward IV, a lusty young giant, who leaps to the throne partly by luck but largely by virtue of his own prowess and the prowess of his supporters. Even when his crown is being taken off and he is being led to imprisonment, he exclaims in supreme self-confidence:

> Yet, Warwick, in despite of all mischance,
> Of thee thyself, and all thy complices,
> Edward will always bear himself as king:
> Though Fortune's malice overthrow my state,
> My mind exceeds the compass of her wheel.
>
> (3 *Henry VI*, IV. iii. 42–46)

It used to be thought that in his 'histories' Shakespeare is mainly interested in giving a running summary of events and in making the scenes follow on without joining them, one to another. But the tendency of recent criticism is to look upon these plays as bound by a moral idea. Wilson Knight, for example, draws attention to the principles of justice and honesty – 'What stronger breastplate than a heart untainted' – which, he thinks, are emphasized in Shakespeare's 2 *Henry VI* and 3 *Henry VI*. 'These', says he, 'dramatize the Wars of the Roses, staging bitter animosities and bloody acts, as rival factions fight, like Lion and Unicorn, for the Crown. Shakespeare here resembles his wild contemporary Christopher Marlowe, but though the events are Marlovian, the treatment is not'.[1] Not only in these two plays but in all the 'histories', there is, on this view, a basic sense of the moral law. But although Shakespeare nowhere supports an upheaval of the moral order, the idea that emerges from these ten dramas, which comprehend so wide a variety of characters and incidents, is of the persistence and abundance of the Spirit of Life. Here a Harry succeeds a Harry, a Nevil a Nevil, a Clifford a Clifford. If the Duke of York is insulted and killed, behind him stand his three sons who are like three suns and two of them are much abler than their father. Queen Margaret, York's relentless foe, is defeated and disgraced, but Shakespeare endows her with exuberant vitality; although she has been likened to a choric Nemesis, she is something more than that. She is not a detached spectator, commenting on the inevitability of retribution, but is personally interested in the destruction of the Yorkists, and thus becomes a symbol of the Spirit of Life which survives defeat and looks beyond death. It is this sense which links the two tetralogies

---

[1] G. Wilson Knight, *The Sovereign Flower* (London, 1958), p. 14.

and connects them with the two remaining plays which seem in other respects to stand apart.

Although individuals are cast off, life marches on. King John, a rapscallion of a king, dies ignominiously, but the Bastard, who is a symbol of irrepressible vitality, lives on to gather together the scattered forces of the English and throw defiance in the face of the invading foreigner. Although Shakespeare does full justice to the magnificent victories of Henry V, he shows that these are only a military and diplomatic adventure, an episode in the great drama of history to be followed by the carnage of the Wars of the Roses, 'Which oft our stage hath shown'. Henry VII brings order and 'smooth-fac'd peace' to a disturbed country, but stability does not mean stagnation. Fortune's wheel continues to revolve as fast as ever before, and *Henry VIII* unrolls before us the tragic procession of Buckingham, Katharine, and Wolsey; if Cranmer escapes for the moment, we also see what thin ice he is skating on. But the supreme lesson to be derived from the historical plays is emphasized here too. Buckingham's tragedy is only an external symptom of a new historical process which will mean the super session of the old nobility by the king and his minister; and the fall of Wolsey and Katharine means the advent of Anne Bullen, out of whose womb will spring Elizabeth, the symbol of New Life, who,

> Though in her cradle, yet now promises
> Upon this land a thousand thousand blessings.
> (V. v. 19–20)

Elizabeth's vitality will, phoenix-like, be renewed in James, who will stand fixed like a star. The times of Elizabeth and James Stuart lie outside the scope of this drama, and Shakespeare does not project his vision into the distant future. That is why he likens James to a fixed star. Inside the play there can be no mistake about the contrast between youthful Anne and the persons ranged against her – the ageing Queen whom she supplants and the aged diplomat whom she, without possibly any effort of her own, helps to pull down. Katharine is virtuous, but has few sparks of vitality, and she cannot give the King what he wants of her – an heir. When Henry says,

> O my lord!
> Would it not grieve an able man to leave
> So sweet a bed-fellow? But, conscience, conscience!

TCG—D

O! 'tis a tender place, and I must leave her,

(II. ii. 141–4)

the indications are quite clear that he transposes the forces that are pulling him in opposite directions. She is no longer a sweet bed-fellow for an able man, and yet conscience feels the hard wrench of parting from a devoted wife. Wolsey is an intrepid but worn-out diplomat, who spins cobwebs of policy in which he is himself entangled. We get only fleeting glimpses of Anne but she is a refreshing contrast to Queen Katharine who has seen her best days and to the wily politician whose glory ripens to rottenness. She is tender, yet impetuous, passionate, yet virtuous, and above all she has the gift of youth which points to the future.

A second quality that characterizes these historical plays may be described as expansiveness. The whirlpool of forces which we call history comprehends all classes of people – not only mighty men but also their wives, lords temporal as well as lords spiritual. Even country squires and still humbler people – whether mob leaders like Jack Cade or a blackguard like Bardolph or the innocent Father who killed his Son and the innocent Son who killed his Father – are caught up in the swirl.

Of the two dominating features of medieval history – Catholicism and feudalism – Shakespeare gives only a one-sided picture of the first, because the powerful prelates who crowd these plays think more of earthly glory than of Christian piety; it has been already pointed out that they are of the tribe of Pope Innocent III and not of St Francis of Assisi. But Shakespeare's kings and barons and their followers are true representatives of European feudal society, of which the principal features, according to Marc Bloch, were: 'A subject peasantry; widespread use of the service tenement (i.e. the fief) instead of a salary, which was out of the question; the supremacy of a class of specialized warriors; ties of obedience and protection which bind man to man and, within the warrior class, assume the distinctive form called vassalage; fragmentation of authority – leading inevitably to disorder . . .'.[1] Shakespeare lays emphasis on the supremacy of a class of specialized warriors and the fragmentation of authority which led inevitably to disorder. In his plays, the barons who are masters of fiefs – the most powerful of them is the Earl of Warwick in *Henry VI* – try to control the king, whom they call God's anointed in name but look

---

[1]Marc Bloch, *Feudal Society* (tr. Manyon, London, 1961), p. 446.

upon as only the first among equals. It is these peers who, as even
the Gardener in *Richard II* knows, weigh the balance in favour of
Bolingbroke, and powerful as he is, Richard III requires the
assistance of Buckingham (and Bourchier) to compass the crown.
When the king is sufficiently strong, he keeps the barons under
his sway, but if he is weak like Henry VI too many people have a
share in the management of the state and then disaster is bound
to follow. The common people, who had little independence,
play generally an ignoble part in historical events. We see the
rowdies maintained by Winchester and Gloucester and there are
bullies and scamps like Pistol and Nym, and not the least interesting specimens of this class are the ragamuffins following Jack
Cade. Although without political status, the commons are not
without political influence or political sense. Ambitious lords
like Bolingbroke or Richard of Gloucester have to woo them and
it is they who haul the Duke of Suffolk to justice. However, what
is most significant about the common people amongst the *dramatis
personae* is that most of them have a *joie de vivre* which gives variety
and richness to the heated animosities and bloody acts which form
the substance of the historical plays. The roisterers who follow
Falstaff are drawn from the London of Shakespeare's day, but there
is no ground for thinking that they had not their prototypes in
medieval society which must have had its own share of loafers and
bullies. Shakespeare's genius lies in endowing them with independence of outlook, sometimes with a distinctive command of
language, and almost always with a good-humoured richness of
perception that enables even the assailants of Clarence and Suffolk
to bandy a joke or an argument before doing away with their
victims.

IV

It is worth while repeating that the greatness of Shakespearian
drama lies chiefly in the revelation of the richness and complexity
of human nature, and this is best realized if we compare the
historical plays with their sources. Coleridge reminds us that in a
historical play 'care must be taken that there appear no dramatic
improbability, as the reality is taken for granted'.[1] Shakespeare
generally reproduces the principal incidents and characters from

---

[1]*Lectures and Notes on Shakespeare*, &c. (World's Classics, No. 363), p. 77.

his sources, but he adds a touch or two which completely transform the wooden figures he has lifted from history. His Richard
III, for example, comes straight from More, Hall and *The True
Tragedie*, but he shades the portrait of the villain in his own way.
In the source books Richard is an instrument of darkness, who
proceeds from crime to crime until he is overtaken by Nemesis.
Shakespeare's Richard, too, is guilty of criminal ambition and as
great a villain as the Richard of the sources, but here his ambition
is only an expression of his vitality which finds an outlet also in
his reckless courage, his artist's capacity for manipulation of
materials, his histrionic gifts and his command of sarcasm, irony,
and a kind of grim humour. It is recorded in the sources that in the
final battle of Bosworth Field, when defeat was imminent,
Richard's followers brought him a swift and light horse to convey
him away, but he, casting away all hope of fortune, success, and
happy chance to come, is said to have answered that on that day
he would make an end of all battles, or else there finish his life.
This is how *The True Tragedie* dramatizes the incident:

> The battel enters Richard *wounded, with his* Page.
>
> King –   A horse, a horse, a fresh horse.
> Page –   A flie my lorde, and save your life.
> King –   Flie villaine, looke I as tho I would flie, no first shall this dull
> and senceless ball of earth receive my body cold and void of
> sence . . . downe is thy sunne Richard . . . yet faint not man,
> for this day if Fortune will, shall make thee king possesst with
> quiet Crown, if Fates deny, this ground must be my grave, yet
> golden thoughts that reach for a Crowne, danted before by
> Fortunes cruell spight, are come as comforts to my drooping
> heart, and bids me keep my Crowne and die a King.[1]

Shakespeare borrows the incident from his sources, but by adding
a touch here and there completely transforms its dramatic
significance:

> Catesby – Rescue, my Lord of Norfolk! rescue, rescue!
> The king enacts more wonders than a man,
> Daring an opposite to every danger:
> His horse is slain, and all on foot he fights,
> Seeking for Richmond in the throat of death.
> Rescue, fair lord, or else the day is lost!

---

[1] *Three Books of Polydore Vergil's English History* (Camden Society Re-print No. XXIX,
1844), p. 225; Hall, op. cit., p. 420; Holinshed, *Chronicles*, III, p. 445; *The True Tragedie
of Richard the Third*, p. 121 (Shak. Lib., 1875, Part II, Vol. I).

Alarum — Enter KING RICHARD.

K. *Rich.*–A horse! a horse! my kingdom for a horse!
Cate. — Withdraw my lord, I'll help you to a horse.
K. *Rich.*–Slave! I have set my life upon a cast,
    And I will stand the hazard of the die.
    I think there be six Richmonds in the field;
    Five have I slain to-day, instead of him. —
    A horse! a horse! my kingdom for a horse!

(V. iv. 1–13)

In Shakespeare's play, although the situation is desperate, Richard is yet unwounded and his vigour is unbedimmed. He has set his life upon a cast, and he wants a horse to help him 'stand the hazard of the die'. But along with his defiant challenge to Fate, there is also the amazed realization, not unmixed with a sense of irony, that the throne to which he has waded through blood and craft should at the most critical hour depend on such a paltry thing as the timely supply of a horse!

Some critics think that the abundance of vitality noticed in Shakespeare's villains – notably in Iago, Richard III, and Falstaff – is a legacy from the Vice in medieval moralities. Referring to the wooing scene (I. ii) in *Richard III*, Bernard Spivack says that it is an amplification 'of the style and method of the typical seduction effected by the Vice in the pivotal scene of the moralities. At such a moment the Vice displays the full extent of his virtuosity. Step by step, with every device at his command, he dissolves his victim's allegiance to virtue and binds him to the evil which he, the Vice, personifies'.[1] But the difference between Shakespeare's Richard III and the medieval Vice is fundamental, for the latter, just because he is a part of an allegorical structure, has no spiritual independence; the hilarity displayed by him is something added to his homiletic function but not organically connected with his character. Shakespeare endows Richard with a resilient personality that reveals but does not exhaust itself in tempting Anne and wearing down her allegiance to virtue. That is the ultimate justification for the liberties Shakespeare takes with time and historical probability. Besides, the winning of Anne is only an artistic exploit which does not seem to serve any practical purpose,

---

[1]Spivack, op. cit., p. 170. Spivack elaborates the connexion between Vice and Iago in Chapters I, II, and XII. Willard Farnham says that 'it is in Falstaff that we have the most complex figure of comedy created by the medieval side of Shakespeare's genius' (*J. Q. Adams Memorial Studies*, Washington, 1948), p. 435.

for Richard does not make clear the 'secret close intent' which his success here will further. It seems that such an adventure gives the best exercise to his faculties in the piping time of peace. Here all the odds are against him, and he overcomes insuperable obstacles by his super-abundant vitality, his lack of moral inhibition, his power of fantastic invention combined with a realistic perception of his victim's weakness. His secret close intent is, like Iago's motive, an after-thought, for like Iago, although to a lesser degree, he too is an artist in crime. Anne's beauty and virtue are a challenge to his abilities, and he only plumes up his will by conquering her as Iago plumes up his by destroying the daily beauty he finds in the lives of Othello, Desdemona, and Cassio. When he has succeeded in his venture, he has forgotten the motive – in fact he had none – and only embroiders his triumph with the flowers of speech:

> Was ever woman in this humour woo'd?
> Was ever woman in this humour won?
> I'll have her; but I will not keep her long.
> What! I, that kill'd her husband, and his father,
> To take her in her heart's extremest hate;
> With curses in her mouth, tears in her eyes,
> The bleeding witness of her hatred by;
> Having God, her conscience, and these bars against me,
> And nothing I to back my suit withal
> But the plain devil and dissembling looks
> And yet to win her, all the world to nothing!
>
> (I. ii. 229–39)

Shakespeare got three facts from his sources: (1) Richard was one of the assailants of Prince Edward; (2) he killed Henry VI in the Tower, and (3) he married Warwick's daughter Anne who had earlier been 'wedded' (or betrothed) to Prince Edward. In the chronicles, although the first two incidents are described in detail, the marriage with Anne is only mentioned and obviously the historians did not find any incongruity in this union. But Shakespeare links these disparate incidents together, paints Anne as a sorrowing widow and the chief mourner of Henry VI, and then makes her fall a victim to Richard's wiles at a time when she has reason to loathe him most. What would be an improbable possibility in fact becomes convincing in fiction, because Richard's character in the play has qualities which make such a strange conquest probable and necessary.

This is the method he adopts in all his historical plays. He reproduces historical incidents with alterations here and there, but although he does not minimize the force of circumstances or of unexpected accidents, his emphasis is on character issuing in action. Not only action but even inaction may reveal subtle shades of personality. Richard of Bourdeaux – a man very different from Richard of Gloucester – was, according to the chronicles, 'prodigall, ambitious and much given to the pleasure of the bodie', but he was 'seemilie of shape and favour & of nature good inough, if the wickednesse & naughtie demeanour of such as were about him had not altered it'. Holinshed ruefully notes that 'hee was a prince unthankfullie used of his subjects', and Froissart records how 'apparelled like a king in his robes of state, his scepter in his hand, and his crown on his head', he dramatically went through the ritual of uncrowning himself.[1] On these slender suggestions Shakespeare bases his portrait of Richard II, making of him both a poet and an actor, whose weakness of character is inwoven into his imaginative and histrionic talents. In the sources Richard is compelled by external forces to yield his crown, but here the initiative comes from his own character. A lotus-eater and a poet, he deposes himself and then enjoys as an artist what he suffers as a man. The historical situation supplied hints for the creation of such a figure, but the conception is entirely Shakespeare's.[2]

Queen Margaret is as indubitably a historical figure as Richard II and Richard III, and her story too has been reproduced with only minor modifications. These modifications, however, transform the chronicle narrative into a moving drama. Her marriage with King Henry VI was negotiated by the Duke (then Earl) of Suffolk, in whose company she first came to England as a bride. As Queen her first business was to dislodge the Duke of Gloucester, who was the Protector of the realm and to take up the reins of government in her hands and in those of her favourites – Suffolk and Somerset. When the Wars of the Roses began, she easily became the leading figure in the Lancastrian camp, but at the end she was defeated, her husband and son were butchered to death, and she herself was bundled off to France. All this is sober history which Shakespeare transfers with but slight alterations to his *Henry VI*. But

---

[1]Holinshed: *Chronicles*, II, pp. 868–9; *The Antient Chronicles of Sir John Froissart* (tr. Bouchier and Berners, London, 1816), IV, p. 587.

[2]It is true that Froissart presents Richard as taking the initiative in surrendering the crown, but he also shows that Richard is helpless. (*Chronicles*, Vol. IV, pp. 570–87).

Margaret is much more alive in Shakespeare's world than in the chronicles, which give an elaborate account of her actions but cannot adequately limn her personality. In the chronicles the Earl of Suffolk is the architect of the marriage, but no reason is assigned for the choice of the bride, though from the diplomatic point of view this marriage was then thought to be 'bothe infortunate and unprofitable'.[1] When the bride was espoused in Tours, there were 'triumphant Justes, costly feastes, and delicate festivities'; there is no mention of Suffolk having played any part in these festivities, though it is reasonable to suppose that he participated in them. Shakespeare's account is much more romantic, although also a little fantastic. Here Margaret is captured by Suffolk in course of a skirmish in France, and she also fascinates her captor. Later on, Margaret confesses that she was captivated by him when in the city of Tours he ran a tilt in honour of her and stole away the ladies' hearts of France. Then it was that she saw Henry's mind in Suffolk's visage.

Shakespeare makes a significant change when he represents the enmity between Margaret and Protector Humphrey in 2 *Henry VI.* All the chroniclers give an account of this enmity but Shakespeare enlivens it by adding to the story of political intrigue the rancour of a personal quarrel between Margaret and Eleanor, Duchess of Gloucester:

> Not all these lords do vex me half so much
> As that proud dame, the Lord Protector's wife:
> She sweeps it through the court with troops of ladies,
> More like an empress than Duke Humphrey's wife.
>
> (I. iii. 78–81)

Later the Duke of York describes her as a tiger's heart wrapped in a woman's hide, but this episode shows that the hide as well as the heart is womanly. Shakespeare portrays in Margaret a woman not as complex and subtle as his later heroines but one gifted with tremendous energy, and even her ghoulishness is an offshoot of her indomitable personality. Describing the Battle of Wakefield, the chroniclers say that the Duke of York, who was both outnumbered and outflanked, lay dead in the field, killed by the Lancastrians. His young son, the Earl of Rutland, was mercilessly killed by Lord Clifford, who, not satisfied with this child-slaughter,

---

[1] Hall's *Chronicle*, p. 205. It should not have been so thought. The proposal marked a realistic approach to the solution of the Anglo-French conflict.

came to the spot where York's corpse lay, and first caused his head to be severed, and then fixing it on a pole presented it to the Queen, who was encamped not far from the scene of battle. In Shakespeare's play, Margaret is herself present on the battle-field, and when York is brought to her a prisoner yet alive, she not only gives him a napkin, dyed in Rutland's blood, but also puts a paper crown on his head to mock his soaring ambition:

> Ay, marry, sir, now looks he like a king!
>
> (3 *Henry VI*, I. iv. 96)

There is a touch of melodrama in all this, but it also brings into prominence the large part played by human passions in the horrors of the Wars of the Roses, which from the purely political point of view had their origin in the contradictions inherent in Feudalism.

The Bastard in *King John* is a semi-historical character; in creating him Shakespeare derived suggestions from all his sources. Holinshed mentions one Philip, King Richard's son, who slew the Viscount of Limoges in revenge of his father's death, and this suggestion could very well be enriched by what Hall says of the Earl of Dunois, who preferred the brand of bastardy to being known as the legitimate son of a cowardly lord: 'my harte geveth me, my noble corage telleth me, that I am the sonne of the noble Duke of Orleaunce, more glad to be his Bastarde, with a mean livying, than the lawfull sonne of that coward cuckolde Cawny with four thousand crounes'.[1] The interweaving of these suggestions was the work of the anonymous playwright who wrote *The Troublesome Raigne of John Kyng of England*, which was in all probability Shakespeare's immediate source and supplied him with all the materials of his plot. But even a superficial comparison of the two works, which are so similar that the source play has been described by some critics as a corrupt version of *King John*, will show that although all the situations and incidents are probably borrowed from *The Troublesome Raigne*, Shakespeare's Faulconbridge is much more complex and possesses more 'blood life' than the sketchy portrait he found in the earlier play. Even the striking first scene in which the Bastard is introduced gives us a clue to the secret of Shakespeare's originality. The Bastard in *The Troublesome Raigne* is undecided whether to claim his patrimony as the legiti-

---

[1] ibid., p. 145.

mate son of Sir Robert Faulconbridge. If he finally accepts bastardy, it is not so much out of conscious willing as under the influence of an all-pervasive 'Eccho', which comes to him in a waking dream:

> Birds in their flight make musicke with their wings,
> Filling the ayre with glorie of my birth:
> Birds, bubbles, leaves, and mountaines, Eccho, all
> Ring in mine eares that I am *Richards* sonne.

> (I. i. 252–5)

This dreamer is transformed into a lusty, good-humoured realist who accepts both the logic of facts and the lure of adventure. He knows and is proud to acknowledge that his 'large composition' is reminiscent more of Coeur-de-Lion's face and tongue than of the thin features of Sir Robert Faulconbridge. Although the prospect of adventure attracts him, he is not a climber or a snob but a realist with a keen awareness of the meanness and corruption of a court life dominated by the principle of Commodity. Even his later idealism is only a philosophy of enlightened self-interest, Commodity transformed into practical patriotism. *The Troublesome Raigne* presents him as a disappointed lover of the King's niece Blanch, who, even when Blanch is married, indulges in the futile hope of making a cuckold of the husband:

> But let the frolicke Frenchman take no scorne,
> If *Philip* front him with an English horne.

> (I. iv. 798–9)

Shakespeare's hero is too 'mounting' in spirit and too large-hearted for amorous dalliance. Indeed, when the proposal of marriage between Lewis and Blanch is made and Lewis whispers to his bride, the Bastard's comment expresses as much cyncism about love as scorn of the lover:

> Drawn in the flattering table of her eye!
> Hang'd in the frowning wrinkle of her brow!
> And quarter'd in her heart! he doth espy
> Himself love's traitor: this is pity now,
> That hang'd and drawn and quarter'd, there should be
> In such a love so vile a lout as he.

> (*King John*, II. i. 504–09)

A patriot, a soldier and a diplomat, he is also gifted with an ebullient sense of humour, which enables him to survey mankind

– himself included – with a measure of detachment. But his cynicism and detachment are mingled with a good-humoured tolerance which enables him to excuse even his mother's adultery. He is no Hamlet sicklied o'er with the pale cast of thought. To him her fault was not her folly. How could a mere woman resist the advances of a man

> Against whose fury and unmatched force
> The aweless lion could not wage the fight?
>
> (I. i. 265–6)

When King John proudly proclaims the prowess of his thirty thousand hearts of 'England's breed' and King Philip of 'As many and as well-born bloods as those', the Bastard jokingly recalls that both the armies, true-bred as they are, contain a fair portion of bastards, too!

Nowhere is Shakespeare's capacity for transforming his sources more in evidence than in his representation of the Bastard's reaction to the death of Prince Arthur, which is the principal theme of the Second Part of *The Troublesome Raigne* and an important episode in *King John*. In the former, the Bastard is tied to the narrow Tudor propaganda of absolute obedience to the king actually on the throne. Even if it be true that King John was responsible for the murder of Prince Arthur, the barons, who are his subjects, have no right to hold an inquisition into his conduct or to go back on their allegiance to him:

> I say tis shame, and worthy all reproofe,
> To wrest such pettie wrongs in tearmes of right,
> Against a King annoynted by the Lord.
> Why *Salsburie*, admit the wrongs are true,
> Yet subjects may not take in hand revenge,
> And rob the heavens of their proper power,
> Where sitteth he to whom revenge belongs.
>
> (II. i. 461–7)

From this hint – if hint it might be called – Shakespeare works out his portrait of the English patriot who places his country above everything else and for whom the reigning king is only a symbol and instrument of the ideal of nationalism. He does not defend John as the Bastard in *The Troublesome Raigne* tries to do – 'For *Arthurs* death King *John* was innocent' (*TR*, II. iii. 457) – and, indeed, pronounces a heavy curse on John's agent Hubert whom he suspects 'very grievously'. The attitude of the other lords only helps him to reach out to his concept of patriotism which is so much wider than mere loyalty to a sovereign. Arthur's death is a pathetic thing; possibly it is the result of a heinous crime. But what amazes him is that for this morsel of dead royalty, for this bare-pick'd bone of majesty, dogged war should be allowed to bristle his angry crest and snarl in the gentle eyes of peace. It is now that he holds forth the image of 'dear mother England', whom John has to protect against 'powers from home and discontents at home'. Thus Commodity is magnified into a principle of large-hearted expediency, and John is transformed into a representative of the nation, who must be great in action as in thought – the real John was great in neither – and although the Bastard is unswerving in his loyalty, his allegiance is not to one who is God's anointed but to the symbol of English unity and liberty. It is in this way that history acquires the spirit, if not the proportions, of a national epic.

Yet another example of Shakespeare's genius for characteriza-tion is seen in his portrait of Jack Cade, derived from Hall's chronicle and probably also from Holinshed's account of the Peasants' Revolt in the reign of Richard II; the anonymous *The Life and Death of Jack Straw* is an interesting 'analogue'. In Hall, Jack Cade is a young man of goodly stature and 'pregnaunt wit', who is enticed to assume the name of John Mortimer and hopes that he will thus be linked to the line of the Earl of March. Suborned by teachers and schoolmasters, he gathers around him a great company of volunteers and raises the standard of revolt. Hall presents him as a subtle leader, 'sober in communication, wyse in disputyng, arrogant in heart and styffe in his opinion'. He allured to him the hearts of the common people by prohibiting Murder, Rape, or Robbery, but he 'tormented of his olde acquayn-tance, lest they should blase and declare his base byrthe, and lowsy lynage'.[1] Holinshed describes Jack Straw, Wat Tyler, and Parson Ball, the leaders of the Peasants' Revolt, as unruly people who are naturally against law and order, and who, in the course of their advance, beheaded all such men of law, justices and jurors as they could lay hands on, alleging that the land should never enjoy her native and true liberty till all those sorts of men were despatched out of the way. They also proposed to burn and destroy all records and evidences and books and writings, demand-

[1] ibid., p. 221.

ing that all warrens, waters and parks and woods be held in common. Preaching equality and liberty, Parson Ball took as his theme the common proverb:

> When Adam delv'd and Eve span,
> Who was then a gentleman?[1]

Shakespeare endows Jack Cade (and some of his men) with abundant high spirits — and what is more significant — with a fertile but fantastic imagination which ignores contradictions and perverts logic. His Jack Cade, like Hall's, lays claim to blue blood, and as a Mortimer he becomes a pretender to the throne, but he is also like Jack Straw, Parson Ball, and Wat Tyler, an apostle of liberty. His royalism both contradicts and enriches his republicanism, for his wit is as simple as a child's, and therefore absolutely untroubled by the irreconcilability of his pretensions. If he is to be a Mortimer, he has to be a knight first and he has no procedural difficulty about the matter: he kneels down, dubs himself a knight, and rises Sir John Mortimer. He is for perfect equality, for the natural liberties of the people, but he himself must be king and in the manner of a feudal suzerain claim tribute from every peer; even more fantastically and perversely he claims the surrender of maidenhead from every woman married in his realm. Hall alleges that he tormented his old acquaintances lest they declare his base lineage, but Shakespeare endows him with a more varied personality. If a Soldier calls him Jack Cade rather than Lord Mortimer, such treason is punished with instantaneous death, but with his friends — Smith and Dick and Holland — he is very informal and they can even indulge in unpalatable 'asides' about his past, provided they openly acknowledge him as their leader and king. He must be worshipped as the supreme lord, but his subjects shall be 'fellow kings', eating and drinking on his score. Hall compliments him and his men on their marching 'in good order of battel',[2] but Shakespeare's Jack Cade is of a different mind. He knows that law and order are an imposition on nature, for he once sealed to a bond and was never his own man again; his followers, therefore, are best in order when they are most out of order. Hall's further testimony that he was sober in communication and wise in dispute would be both true and false of the interesting figure drawn by Shakespeare, for our standards of

---

[1]*Chronicles*, II, p. 749. There is an elaborate description of 'the rebellion of the commons' on pp. 735–51.
[2]Hall's *Chronicle*, p. 220.

sobriety and wisdom are inoperative in his world. He is wonderfully self-possessed – one may call him sober in that sense – and he
has a logic of his own which is irrefutable because it is unreal.
France is the enemy of England, and since French is the language of
France, the conclusion is irresistible that an Englishman who
knows French must be an enemy of England too. It is because
learned men have corrupted our understanding with academic
logic that we are tempted to detect a fallacy in such excellent
argument. His logic is, indeed, as original as his political philosophy; he affirms his claim to blue blood by referring to his father's
occupation, and argues back from the present to the past. It is
supposed that the Earl of March's true heir was stolen away by a
beggar-woman, and ignorant of his birth and parentage he became
a bricklayer; there is no doubt that Jack Cade's father was a
bricklayer and Smith the Weaver can testify that the bricks with
which this bricklayer built a chimney in his father's house are
alive to this day – and this is an incontrovertible proof that Jack
Cade is a Mortimer! Sometimes logic and law are twisted in
support of his condemnation of the government he wants to
overthrow. By virtue of a privilege known as benefit of clergy,
men who knew how to read and write could claim certain
immunities when prosecuted for crimes. What was an exemption
for those who could read and write is interpreted by Jack Cade as
a special device deliberately invented to harass innocent poor
men: 'Thou hast appointed justices of peace, to call poor men
before them about matters they were not able to answer. Moreover thou hast put them in prison; and because they could not read
thou hast hanged them; when indeed only for that cause they
have been most worthy to live'. (2 *Henry VI*, IV. vii. 45–51).

Jack Cade's perverse logic, his strange politics in which
absolute autocracy coheres with perfect democracy, and his
anarchical economy which will bring plenty without industry
and without the use of money – these are not disparate traits
clumsily assembled together but emanations from his peculiar
personality. He is not sober but nonchalant, not wise but ingenious,
not stiff but absurd. With his inventive genius, he has created a
fantastic world where his impulses and wishes are laws, and that
is why he can achieve miracles in a chaotic situation. But the real
world of order and common sense asserts itself in the persons of
Buckingham and Clifford, and his first reaction is one of dismayed
surprise. The multitude is blown away from him like a feather,

and he has no alternative but flight. Even flight, however, is no protection, for he is killed by Alexander Iden. But to the last he retains his high spirits, proudly claiming that he was vanquished by famine, not by superior valour, and exhorting all the world to be cowards!

Jack Cade's story is a minor item in Hall's account but it is a major episode in Shakespeare's 2 *Henry VI*. He even fills it out with tit-bits borrowed from Holinshed's account of the reign of Richard II. In all these historical plays the emphasis is on the personal, human aspect of events, on the conflict and clash of Nature and Fortune in the lives of men and women. This explains the importance assigned without historical warrant to women – to Eleanor Cobham, Duchess of Gloucester, to Richard II's Queen, to Kate Percy, wife of Hotspur, who are all historical characters but play a part in the dramas for which there is no support in history. Not only have such characters an interest of their own but they also help to throw light on more important figures like Richard II, Humphrey, Duke of Gloucester, Queen Margaret, and Hotspur. Dowager Queen Elinor, King John's mother, and Constance, mother of Prince Arthur, are made more prominent in Shakespeare's drama than could be accounted for by considerations of historical veracity. Indeed, it has been noted by many critics that Shakespeare, who in *King John* ignores the Magna Carta, accords to the episode of Prince Arthur such an exaggerated importance that history has been thrown out of focus. He gives a more or less faithful account of historical incidents in *Richard II* and *Richard III*, but in these plays too the centre of interest is not the historical narrative but the character of the protagonist, and the gift for poetry displayed by Richard II is a dramatic invention. In *Richard II* and *Richard III*, Nature and Fortune are so inextricably intermingled that in spite of adherence to history these plays are more like tragedies than histories. Shakespeare portrays Henry V as a man of action, a symbol of English nationalism or Jingoism, but more importance is attached to the purely personal aspects of the King's character than to his dashing victories. Even the minor episodes of Horner and Peter in 2 *Henry VI* and of Fluellen and Williams in *Henry V* have more than a diversionary value, for they help to throw history in perspective by showing how the soaring ambitions and mighty deeds of kings and barons impinge on the lives of ordinary people.

Henry IV in its two parts is generally looked upon as Shake-

speare's greatest achievement in this genre, and one reason why
it is so honoured is the presence of Sir John Falstaff, who is only
remotely connected with history. Falstaff is one of Shakespeare's
most famous creations, and we are so much accustomed to looking
upon him as a character in comedy that we lose sight of his
importance in the context of a historical drama. Indeed, there are
critics who think that the comic episodes usurp a place in this
drama which should rightfully belong to historical events. 'The
plays of Henry IV', says Schelling, 'especially the second one –
are wanting in incident and the substitution of an interest in
character, however absorbing, in the main historical thread and
in the interwoven strand of comedy, by no means suffices to
remedy this defect'.[1] The significance of Henry IV as a historical
drama and the implications of the above criticism will be considered in a later chapter. What it is necessary to point out here
is that the comic episodes centring on Falstaff are not to be looked
upon as remedying the paucity of historical incidents. Rather
they throw light on the historical incidents and enlarge the
perspective in which such incidents are to be viewed. The impact
of political events is felt not only by great barons but also by humble
people, not merely by men of honour like Hotspur but also by
men without honour like Falstaff, and wars are fought not only by
fiery Douglases but also by contemptible scamps like Thomas Wart
and Mouldy Mike. Mighty events which immediately concern the
men at the top have an enlarging effect on the lives of the people
of the lower classes – Nym and Pistol and Mistress Quickly and
Doll Tearsheet – who are caught up in the vortex of history, and
thus comedy finds its proper place in a structure that has the
largeness of an epic.

---

[1] F. E. Schelling, The English Chronicle Play (New York, 1902), p. 122.

CHAPTER THREE

The First Tetralogy

I

SHAKESPEARE makes a survey of the history of England from the last years of the reign of Richard II to the death of Richard III in eight dramas which may be divided into two tetralogies, with *King John* and *Henry VIII* serving as the Prologue and Epilogue. Of the two tetralogies, the later period covering the reigns of Henry VI, Edward IV and Richard III, was taken up first in four plays which belong to the early period of Shakespeare's career. In the second tetralogy, *Richard II*, though not an early play, is too lyrical to be fully dramatic, and *Henry V* shows Shakespeare as still taking a 'complaisant' view of life, but the two parts of *Henry IV* are different, for here he not only presents a section of history but also explores its significance. These plays question assumptions and juxtapose values, and here although the dramatic structure is of comic history there is a foretaste of the 'daemonic' Shakespeare who would soon be at work on the tragedies and the dark comedies.

The constituent plays of the tetralogies are independent works, but they are also related to the other plays in the series in which they occur and a study of one tetralogy is enriched by an awareness of the other. The Epilogue to *Henry V* refers to the catastrophic reign of Henry VI, and Henry V has visibly grown out of Prince Hal of *Henry IV*, who is first referred to, somewhat irrelevantly, towards the end of *Richard II*. There are other links which are more emphatic, and such links, placed in appropriate contexts, show that all these plays from 1 *Henry VI* to *Henry V*, although separate entities, are parts of a wider organism which, with the support of *King John* and *Henry VIII*, gives us Shakespeare's vision of history. Not only do these eight plays form a single whole, but there is, in spite of differences in conception and style between the first tetralogy and the second, continuous development from one play to another, even from the First Part of *Henry VI* to the

Second and the Third, although there are critics who think that the later parts of *Henry VI* were composed earlier than the First.[1] Shakespeare streamlines the narrative by reducing the profusion of incidents, gradually shifts the emphasis from plot to character and interweaves character to an emergent idea. In 1 *Henry VI*, there are two prominent personalities – Joan and Talbot – but it is primarily a chronicle of incidents – true and invented, ranging from the death of Henry V to the marriage of Henry VI and Margaret of Anjou. In the Second Part, the centre of interest is the quarrel between Humphrey, Duke of Gloucester and his enemies, which soon broadens into the mightier conflict of York and Lancaster which occupies the Third Part. In these two plays, greater respect is shown to history than in the First Part, but what is more important dramatically is that the focus of interest definitely shifts from the chronicling of events to the portraiture of dominant personalities, and *Richard III*, the final play of the series, although it gives a slice of English history, concentrates on the personal tragedy of a villain who is an exponent of Machiavellism. There is in all these early plays an increasing tendency to simplify the network of history and to trace historical changes to the unpredictable element in human character. Not that there is any anticipation of the intricacy and depth of the later tragedies, but there can be no doubt about Shakespeare's conception or method. The characters are black and white sketches rather than delicately shaded polychromes, but history is shown as primarily a representation of the movements they initiate, and Richard III, the greatest of them, though drawn neither subtly nor profoundly, has a varied intellectual armoury with which he wears down opposition, and his ultimate failure is not merely a personal tragedy but the defeat of a philosophy.

Two examples taken from 1 *Henry VI*, which have already been cited in another context, will throw light on how Shakespeare's genius began to work on the cumbrous materials supplied by history. When Henry V died in 1422, the key to the situation lay

---

[1]For example, Dover Wilson (Introduction to 1 *Henry VI* in New Cambridge Shakespeare, 1952, pp. ix–xiii) argues plausibly that 'whereas 1 *Henry VI* was written by a person or persons who knew all about 2 *Henry VI*, and I think 3 *Henry VI* also, those two plays display complete ignorance of the drama which ostensibly precedes them', and he points out many 'signs' in support of his contention. In all Shakespeare's plays, there are many loose ends and minor discrepancies which may be advanced for or against any hypothesis. A critically safer course would be to rely on the total significance rather than on the presumption created by minor details. The general impression produced by these plays is that there is progressive development from the beginning to the middle and from the middle to the end.

in the attitude of the powerful Duke of Burgundy. 'And as touching the estate of my realmes', said Henry V on his death-bed, 'Fyrst I commaund you to love and joyne together in one leage or concord and in one unfained amitie, kepying continuall peace and amitie with Philip Duke of Burgoyn'.[1] The defection of Burgundy was due to many causes, not the least among them being the marriage of Duke Humphrey to Jacqueline of Hainault, the death of the Burgundian princess Anne, the first Duchess of Bedford, and Bedford's subsequent marriage to the sister of the Count of St Pol. Not that Hall, and, following Hall, Holinshed give a clear analysis of the tortuous workings of historical forces, but they do point out the complexity of the situation and the mixed motives that swayed Burgundy. But Shakespeare does not enter into this tangled web at all. Introducing a flagrant departure from history, he makes Joan, who died some years before the Burgundian defection and was indeed herself captured by the Burgundians, appeal successfully to the patriotic instincts of the renegade:

> See, see the pining malady of France;
> Behold the wounds, the most unnatural wounds,
> Which thou thyself hast giv'n her woeful breast.
>
> (III. iii. 49–51)

Burgundy is 'bewitch'd' and 'vanquished' and transfers his loyalty to the French side. This is a travesty of history and not very good drama, but it gives a clear indication of Shakespeare's method.

Our second example is equally suggestive. Suffolk negotiated the marriage of Henry VI and Margaret of Anjou as a diplomat; he did not make her a captive in battle. This marriage was generally unpopular and particularly hateful to the Duke of Gloucester, who wanted a more prosperous alliance. But in the state of affairs then prevailing, it was a stroke of realism, for it was calculated to bring peace when the English were losing one French possession after another; even Hall says that it was 'an honorable truce, for the safeguard of Normandy, and the wealth of the realm', but as he was no friend of the Lancastrians, he suggests baser motives too, although he is not sure whether Suffolk was corrupted with riches or too fondly 'affectionate to this unprofitable marriage'.[2] Shakespeare all but lifts this episode out of the context of history and invents a romance of chivalry in which Suffolk is the knight-errant and Margaret his sovereign

---

[1]Hall's *Chronicle*, p. 112; also Holinshed, *Chronicles*, p. 132.
[2]*Hall's Chronicle*, p. 204.

lady; the only link that this romantic invention has with Hall's narrative is that the marriage causes sore annoyance to Humphrey and thus prepares the ground for the bitter rivalries portrayed in 2 *Henry VI*. Such simplification, however, is not a characteristic of historical drama alone. History itself has to give a truncated, mutilated account of events which, when they occurred, were due to causes that contemporaries could not assess correctly and did not record faithfully and completely. Shakespeare, even in his earliest drama, cuts through the enormous mass of historical record, and re-creates the past as a story of human passion, in which all that is intricate or baffling is to be traced to the enigma of human character.

II

The First Part of *Henry VI*, which is probably the earliest of these plays, takes so many liberties with the chronicle account of historical incidents that Bullough calls it 'a fantasia on historical themes' rather than a historical drama.[1] It is supposed to begin in 1422 when Henry V is just dead and has yet to be interred, but this single scene lumps together events that are separated by more than a decade. Here there are references to the loss of French possessions, which happened many years after Henry V's death, including that of Paris which was occupied by the French in 1436. Bedford prepares to go with ten thousand men to France to strengthen the siege of Orleans, but this occurred midway between Henry's death and the loss of Paris – in 1428–9, and it was about this time, not when Henry was just dead, that the Dauphin was crowned in Rheims; the scene ends with Winchester's proceeding to place himself in charge of the young King at Eltham – a step he took in 1425. There is scarcely any other scene in a historical drama in which so many liberties have been taken with historical time. Not only is time telescoped and chronology turned topsy-turvy but the account of historical events is mixed with a good deal of invention. We hear of the defeat and imprisonment of Talbot, which did not occur until several years later, and the whole account of Talbot is a curious mixture of fact and fiction. After a long and distinguished career in France and Ireland, Talbot re-joined the Anglo-French war in 1427, took part in the siege of Orleans, was defeated and taken prisoner at Patay in 1429, and was not ransomed till 1431. He

---

[1]Bullough, *Narrative and Dramatic Sources of Shakespeare*, Vol. III, 1960, p. 25.

recovered Bourdeaux in 1452 and was killed in 1453, twenty-two years after the burning of Joan La Pucelle, whom Shakespeare represents as his chief antagonist in 1 *Henry VI*. There is no evidence that these two mighty figures ever met, and the only connexion historically between them was that Talbot was present at the siege of Orleans which Joan helped to raise. Joan's fighting career was, indeed, very short. She appeared on the scene in 1429 and was captured by the Burgundians and the English about a year later. This is far removed from Suffolk's negotiating the French marriage of Henry VI in 1444–5. As pointed out before, Shakespeare's account of the negotiations is largely fictitious; Suffolk was old enough to be Margaret's father and in his diplomatic mission he was accompanied by his wife. There are other violations of history equally flagrant. The meeting of Joan with Charles and his bout with her are not according to record. The episode of the Countess of Auvergne is a dramatic invention, and so is the meeting at the Temple Garden, which bears on it the unmistakable stamp of Shakespearian authorship. There is also no historical evidence for the talk between Mortimer and Richard Plantagenet in the Tower. The recovery of Orleans, which is modelled on the re-capture of La Mans, is wishful dramatic thinking. Rouen was not lost until 1449 and never re-taken. Burgundy's desertion of the English cause occurred about four years after the death of Joan, who could have had nothing to do with it, and Charles did not accept terms of peace as he is made to do at the end of the play.

Yet in spite of the violence done to history, it would be a mistake to regard the play as a mere fantasia. Although the dramatist departs from the historical sequence and lumps to-gether far-fetched events and introduces episodes for which there is no authority, the representation is not unhistorical in substance. First of all, Shakespeare correctly envisages the spirit and atmo-sphere of the times – the personal heroism and headlong courage of feudal barons, their ambitions and intrigues, the terror inspired by Talbot and the irrepressible nationalism of the French, of which Joan was the symbol. Even the fictitious episode of the Countess of Auvergne correctly reflects the life of the English on foreign soil – the amours of lusty young men with French ladies, the risks such amours involved, and Talbot's resourcefulness and courage for which the French dreaded him so much that mothers would lull their children to sleep, crying, 'A Talbot! A Talbot!' The principal theme of 1 *Henry VI* is the loss of the French possessions, ending with the negotiations of marriage between Henry VI and Margaret. In the course of this long warfare, victory sometimes came to one party and sometimes to the other. As Hall remarks: 'Thus ladye victory sometyme smiled on the English part, and sometyme on the Frenche side. Thus one gayned this daie, and lost on the nexte. Thus Fortune chaunged, and thus chaunce happened, accordyng to the olde proverbe, saiyng, in war is nothyng certain, and victory is ever doubtfull'.[1]

In Shakespeare's play victories 'are whirled like a potter's wheel', and he does not care if the details are mostly incorrect. On the English side the leading figure was Talbot and on the French side Joan. So it is not untrue to the spirit of history, though it may be a departure from fact, if the two doughty champions are made to fight each other, and Joan who was burnt in 1431 is seen jeering at the corpse of Talbot, who died twenty-two years after her. In history as well as in Shakespeare's play, the decline of the English set in after Henry V's death, and Talbot's death meant the end of English adventurism in France; but in the play the story becomes more probable because Suffolk's peaceful diplomacy follows Talbot's exit from the stage. Two landmarks in this downward process were the deaths of Salisbury and Bedford, and Shakespeare, following Hall, gives due prominence to both. A very important factor of French success was Burgundy's defection, but more vital than any other force was resurgent French nationalism, the alacrity with which the French threw off the English yoke and re-asserted their allegiance to the Dauphin, although for Hall, who frequently mentions such changes of side, this was a symptom of French falsity, treachery or perversity, especially because under the English the common people knew liberties which they forfeited as soon as they went back to French rule. It is of this nationalist sentiment that Joan, as Shaw would show later on, was the champion, and although Burgundy's return to French allegiance was due to purely personal causes, the fact remains that Joan did write to Burgundy, urging him to join the side with which he had natural affinity. By a stroke of historical imagination Shakespeare endows Burgundy with the nationalism which, running counter to feudal loyalties, swayed the French people and was the main factor of the Dauphin's success. Thus although Shakespeare treats historical details in a bewildering way and the treatment is more episodic than dramatic, he pre-

---

[1]Hall's *Chronicle*, p. 197.

serves the essence of history intact, giving us what Bernard Shaw calls 'A true history that never happened',[1] or happened very perfunctorily.

Immature as the play is, critics have found in it a central meaning in the light of which the multifarious incidents may be organized. According to Tillyard, the dominant theme of the tetralogy is order: 'Behind all the confusion of civil war, and the more precious and emphatic because of the confusion, is the belief that the world is a part of the eternal law and that earthly mutability, as in Spenser's last cantos, is itself a part of a greater and permanent pattern'.[2] Tillyard supports his thesis, so far as the first part of *Henry VI* is concerned, by referring to the very first words of the play, in which Bedford speaks of 'bad revolting stars', and then also to the homage paid by Talbot to Henry VI at the time of the French coronation of the English monarch. These, however, are two stray speeches in which the idea of order and pattern is only remotely suggested. Bedford's words are nothing but an extravagant expression of grief as Talbot's speech is just a vassal's homage to his lord. To read a philosophical meaning into either of them would be to ignore their contextual significance, and to make them the repository of Shakespeare's total meaning would be to throw the rest of the play out of focus. Indeed, there is so much of angry brawling and violent recrimination that J. P. Brockbank looks upon the Henry VI plays as a dramatization of the Frame of Disorder and the first part as a pageantry of dissension.[3] Reese thinks that in this tetralogy Shakespeare 'attempts the orthodox reconciliation between a providential view of history and the conviction that man, while not the total author of his fate, does by his own actions co-operate in his destiny'.[4] After Henry IV's crime, of which a detailed account is given by Mortimer in 1 *Henry VI*, II. v, the English – although Mortimer himself does not draw this lesson – are foredoomed, and it is no wonder that Talbot, in spite of his heroism, is helpless, for he and his soldiers fight for 'a cause which the higher powers have already destined to defeat'.[5] Henry VI is a good man, but he too, on this view, is partly responsible, for he chooses the wrong bride. This interpretation, like Till-

[1]Subtitle to *In Good Charles's Golden Days* (Standard Edition, London, 1946). The original subtitle was: '*a history lesson*' (1939).
[2]*Shakespeare's History Plays*, p. 150.
[3]*Early Shakespeare*, pp. 73–100.
[4]*The Cease of Majesty*, p. 166.
[5]ibid., p. 172.

yard's, is too narrowly didactic for Shakespeare's portraiture to
fit into it. Mortimer, in the scene referred to, does indeed speak
of Henry IV's original crime of deposing and murdering the
rightful king, but he also tells his nephew how Henry V added to
his father's crime by beheading the Earl of Cambridge who
wanted to give the throne to Richard's rightful heir. In this play,
there is no reference to the French gold which Henry V thought
corrupted Cambridge and his associates. Whatever the Earl's
motive might have been, the suppression of the Mortimers was
an act of 'bloody tyranny',[1] for which on any moral interpretation
of history Henry V deserved to suffer and did not. Shakespeare's
portraiture, which is aesthetic and dramatic, represents every
point of view, that of the Lancastrians as well as of the Yorkists,
of Henry V as well as of Mortimer, of the English as well as of
the French.

Brockbank looks upon 1 *Henry VI* as a pageantry of dissension,
and the description is correct. Only we must remember that
Shakespeare emphasizes the processional aspect as well as the
spectacular; that is to say, he portrays a world that is not merely
large and dazzling but also in continual flux. If the details of
history have been re-arranged and facts have been embroidered
with fiction, these modifications seem primarily to have been
made to bring out this idea of ceaseless movement, of the evolution
of one kind of dissension into another. The old feudal order in
which kings could claim territories in other countries is succeeded
by a new order – equally feudal – in which barons try to rule both
the king and his kingdom. Salisbury and Bedford are representatives of the chivalry of an age that is passing away; they are being
superseded by men like York and Somerset who have different
ambitions and attitudes. The Temple Garden scene, a dramatic
invention, marks the onset of new forces, new ambitions and
alignments. Talbot's career furnishes another clue to this change.
When the play opens he is hefty and vigorous and young enough to
receive an assignation from a lady; above all, he is a sturdy fighter
for his king. Towards the end of the play he is a worn out old man,
the victim of the intrigues of a new generation of barons who
think more of their own interests than of the king whom they are
expected to serve. In the opening scene of 2 *Henry VI*, Gloucester
protests along with Warwick and York against the surrender of

---

[1] It started with John of Gaunt, who, in order to bar Philippa and her children, argued in
Parliament that the succession descended only through males.

the French heritage of the English king. But their tone – very different from that of the lords in the first scene of 1 *Henry VI* – is elegiac and not militant; they only bewail the passing away of a heroic age they are powerless to recall. Gloucester and Suffolk, and York and Somerset will soon be enmeshed in the toils of power politics and Henry V's French victories will be no more than an echo from a buried past.

1 *Henry VI*, which has a sprawling plot with four themes, may be regarded as a drama without a hero, but it contains two colourful figures – Joan and Talbot, who are in the forefront in the first four acts of the play, and it is because they are not seen in the Fifth Act that this portion appears to be an afterthought. Of these two mighty figures, Joan, though less important, may be considered first, because Shakespeare's delineation of her has been the subject of more than one controversy. First, it seems that there are two portraits here, and they are irreconcilable. Shakespeare's Joan of Arc is at the same time a holy virgin and a strumpet, a divinely inspired patriot and a fiendish witch, a prophetess and a liar. Such incompatibility, more than anything else, supports the theory of composite authorship, which has been hotly debated by generations of scholars. It is possible that the libellous part of the portrait was an inferior dramatist's work which Shakespeare touched up but could not wholly transform. Or, since the scenes of denigration occur towards the end of the play, it may be that Shakespeare at first conceived a heroic Maid of Orleans and then blackened her to satisfy the prejudices of his audience. In history, as in literature, Joan is a puzzling figure. She was a simple, ingenuous shepherd girl, who performed miracles, but the miracles are capable of a rational explanation. Although unacquainted with the ways of civilized society, she put to silence ministers and bishops, and as an ignorant shepherd girl of seventeen she led the French armies to victory. Although full records of her life and death by burning are now available, the mystery of her genius and character remains unsolved. Andrew Lang portrays her as a capable general, but cannot explain the fundamental puzzle of how, without military background, training and experience, she came to be a general at all. Anatole France has written a fascinating account of her career, but although he claims to have restored the Maid to life and humanity, in his biography Joan is denuded of every positive virtue, and one wonders if she was anything more than an instrument or a stooge of priests and

generals. A benevolent sceptic, he has depicted a tender woman without a shred of the personality which bore down opposition and swept the dispirited and panic-stricken French army to triumph. Bernard Shaw, who has written possibly the most famous work on Joan, looks upon her as an unconscious rationalist, but his portrait too is one-sided, because he fails to recapture the mystical element in Joan's character, drawing her mainly as a brilliant example and a half-conscious exponent of the philosophy of Creative Evolution. Both Anatole France and Bernard Shaw emphasize the sharp contrasts in Joan's character: 'She was a warrior, and she was kind; she was an illuminate, and she was sensible, she was a woman of the people, and a good knight; in the sacred fairy-tale which is her history, the shepherdess becomes a handsome Saint Michael' (Anatole France).[1] Bernard Shaw sums up the paradox by saying that 'there were only two opinions about her. One was that she was miraculous: the other was that she was unbearable'.[2]

Neither Bernard Shaw nor Anatole France is a Shakespeare, but if these two men of genius in the twentieth century, with all the materials which modern research has placed at their command, have failed to give a satisfactory account of this puzzling shepherd girl, we cannot expect Shakespeare, who did not have before him the fruits of modern scholarship and who had to pander to the tastes of his audience, to give us a convincing and adequate portrait. What is remarkable is that crude and scurrilous as his account of Joan is, he succeeds in laying his finger on the most significant traits in Joan's character – her faith in the rightness of the cause of nationalism and her realistic appraisal of the value of idealism in practical life. When on the eve of introducing her to Charles, the Bastard says:

> The spirit of deep prophecy she hath,
> Exceeding the nine sybils of old Rome;
> What's past and what's to come she can descry,
>
> (I. ii. 55–57)

his words have a deeper significance than he is aware of. The past belonged to the cruel foe and to the unpatriotic Frenchman who inflicted unnatural wounds on his own country. Her own remedy is simple:

---

[1]*On Life and Letters* (tr. D. B. Stewart): Third Series (London, 1922), p. 239.
[2]Preface to *Saint Joan*.

> God's mother deigned to appear to me,
> And in a vision full of majesty
> Will'd me to leave my base vocation
> And free my country from calamity:
>
> (ibid. 78–81)

She, too, *wills* Charles, the Bastard, and others to drive the English away from their common country which belongs to them and not to the invading foreigner. When events take an adverse turn, her will-force comes into play, and she puts new strength into the drooping spirits of Frenchmen. When Reignier timidly asks if they will surrender Orleans, she administers a sharp rebuke:

> Why, no, I say, distrustful recreants!
> Fight till the last gasp; I will be your guard.
>
> (ibid. 126–7)

When after the loss of Rouen – for which there is no historical warrant – the princes are seized with dismay, and she is asked to search out her wit for some secret policies, she herself proposes a measure which is obviously appropriate but which nobody would think feasible. The situation can be retrieved if Burgundy deserts his foreign ally. He must be *willed* back to the French fold. She does 'bewitch' him, but only by making a simple appeal to the patriotic sentiment which will be the dominating sentiment of the future and replace baronial ambitions by democracy and nationalism.

The heroic Talbot is the most important character in the play. We have the contemporary testimony of Nashe that it was his exploits, occupying about three quarters of the play, which drew large audiences, and amongst modern critics Tillyard is inclined to call this part of the tetralogy the *Tragedy of Talbot*.[1] Talbot is a Titan, both on the field and off it, and Shakespeare draws a very grand picture of the intrepid warrior whose name was a terror to the French. But the portrait is too flamboyant to be quite human. The colours are laid on too garishly, and although Shakespeare tries here and there to reveal the man behind the heroic mask, there is neither subtlety nor psychological development. Bernard Shaw complains that Shakespeare's heroes are not 'self-acting';[2] if there is any leading character in the whole range of Shakespearian drama who is open to this charge it is Talbot. Even when

[1] *Shakespeare's History Plays*, p. 163.
[2] *Man and Superman*: Epistle Dedicatory.

he urges his son to save his life by flight, it is the English scourge of France more than an anxious father that speaks:

> Fly, to revenge my death when I am dead;
> The help of one stands me in little stead.
> O! too much folly is it, well I wot,
> To hazard all our lives in one small boat.
> If I to-day die not with Frenchmen's rage,
> To-morrow I shall die with mickle age:
> By me they nothing gain an if I stay;
> 'T is but the short'ning of my life one day.
> In thee thy mother dies, our household's name,
> My death's revenge, thy youth, and England's fame.
>
> (IV. vi. 30–39)

Talbot's exploits take up a disproportionately large space when the three parts of *Henry VI* are considered as forming a single unit. It is not improbable that the first draft – whosoever made it – was designed as a play of French warfare with Talbot as the hero. But as the larger theme dawned on Shakespeare, he subordinated Talbot's tragedy to it, although this meant a flagrant departure from history. The leading theme of the three plays on *Henry VI* is the catastrophic result of civil strife; it is broached in the opening scene of 1 *Henry VI*, it comes suddenly and vividly to life in the Temple Garden scene, and all the other episodes are subsumed under it. Shakespeare displays remarkable constructional skill by trying to re-write history in the interests of drama. Talbot's death in 1453 brought the Hundred Years' War to a close, and in this play too it draws the curtain over the French adventure set on foot by Henry V. The negotiations of Henry VI's marriage with a French Princess come, therefore, appropriately after Talbot's death, and not, as in history, before it. What is equally important is that taking a hint from the chronicle account that Talbot's defeat was due to inferiority in numbers and deficiency in supply, Shakespeare connects this inadequacy with the personal animosities of York and Somerset, and thus the Talbot episode, long as it is, becomes a vital part of the main theme of the tetralogy – the evils of civil dissension.

The keynote is struck in the very first scene of 1 *Henry VI*, where Messenger after Messenger announces the swift loss of French possessions, somewhat prophetically, because in the later scenes we find that Paris and Rouen are still in the hands of the English, and the siege of Orleans has not yet been raised. The cause of these disasters is said to be the maintenance of several factions in England, a sample of which is provided by the wordy brawling between two leading figures – Humphrey, Duke of Gloucester and the (Cardinal) Bishop of Winchester. The brawling becomes more heated in the third scene, where from words their followers take to blows, and the Mayor has difficulty in preserving peace in the city. Up to this point it is largely a story of personal rivalry at Court, but suddenly there is a flaring up of jealousies and rivalries which will soon rage over the whole of England. Dramatically, the most effective episode is that of the plucking of the roses in the Temple Garden and part of its effectiveness lies in its abruptness. One does not know when and at what spot a simmering volcano will erupt. In the Temple Garden, the lords quarrel over a legal nicety which is too insignificant to be mentioned. But the next scene presents an important political issue that will divide them into two warring camps. The dying Mortimer convinces Richard Plantagenet of his indubitable title to the throne and Richard begins to look beyond the immediate squabbles to a larger venture. Both these scenes are unhistorical, but they re-capture the spirit and atmosphere of history, and in them the past comes to life in the heated animosities of warring lords and in the lingering ambition of a frustrated pretender to the throne. The King takes three false steps which help to kindle the smouldering fires of faction and discontent. He confers a Dukedom on Richard Plantagenet without any idea of the consequences of his mistaken generosity, and while thus raising Plantagenet he even more thoughtlessly wears a red rose, the badge of Plantagenet's enemy Somerset. What is worse, having no insight into the situation that is developing, he puts these jarring lords in joint command of the operation in France. The result of this last foolish move is at once seen in the disasters that overtake Talbot and the British army – the first of the 'ill events' foretold, once again without historical warrant, by the aged Duke of Exeter.

In the Fifth Act it is clearly stated that the French wars are ended, and a new drama of power politics will begin. We were given a glimpse of Suffolk's character in the Temple Garden scene, where he plainly said that his will should be law:

> Faith, I have been a truant in the law,
> And never yet could frame my will to it;
> And therefore frame the law unto my will.

(II. iv. 7–9)

He appears three times after this when the war is going on – in III. i, iv and IV. i – but on all these occasions he is a spectator rather than active participant. Obviously he has been silently garnering wisdom from the squabbles of others, and in the Fifth Act he comes to the forefront to win a bride for his King, for he realizes that the best way to rule the factions is first to rule the King through the Queen. The last words in the play are his, and they are characteristic:

> Margaret shall now be queen, and rule the king;
> But I will rule both her, the king, and realm.
>
> (V. v. 107–08)

In order to give this new direction, Shakespeare adopts many devices, which although somewhat clumsy leave no doubt about his intention. The episode is not without historical justification, for there was indeed an abortive Peace Conference in 1435, and marriage between Henry VI and one of the daughters of the Earl of Armagnac was proposed in 1442 as a move calculated to end the hostilities between the two countries. But the peace concluded in V. iv of this drama where Charles accepts the terms which in history he rejected in 1435 is fictitious; its only link with history is a conference that brought about a short truce in 1444 and with it the marriage of Henry to the daughter of Reignier. It seems that Shakespeare is anxious to end his dramatization of the French War, which, in spite of all the prominence given to it, is only an episode, and he now takes up the thread of his principal theme – the Wars of the Roses – in which Margaret as Queen of England will play a leading role.

In handling the theme of marriage, Shakespeare simplifies the incidents in order to be able to throw light on the significance of human relationships. The marriage was proposed by the Duke of Orleans and supported by the Beauforts and then pushed through by Suffolk. Shakespeare, following Hall, makes Suffolk alone responsible for it but adds one or two touches for which there are only faint suggestions in his source. Hall describes Suffolk as 'too much affectionate to this unprofitable marriage', alleging that he might have been corrupted by bribes; or it might be that Suffolk thought that such an alliance would safeguard Normandy. Shakespeare ignores the political motive or the suggestion of bribery. In his version Suffolk is attached to the match because he becomes fond of the bride, and he hopes that such a marriage will herald an era of peace and also power and authority for himself. Following up a suggestion by Hall that Suffolk was 'the Quenes dearlynge',[1] Shakespeare builds up a romantic story that will be woven into the sordid squabbles of the factious barons. It will not only spell disaster for Suffolk but set ablaze a civil war in which England will long be mad and scar herself, and brother will blindly shed brother's blood, the father his son's and the son his sire's.

III

A. W. Ward says that the First Part of *Henry VI* produces an impression of 'crowding, clamour and confusion'.[2] The Second Part affects us differently. It is as crowded and clamorous as the First, but largely free from confusion. The scenes are all laid in England, and there is a clear line of development from the beginning to the middle and from the middle to the end, with the middle — the murder of the Duke of Gloucester — coming half way through in the Third Act. In the First Part, Talbot, who has been acclaimed as the hero by some critics, is only incidentally connected with the plot; his death at Bourdeaux coincides with the end of the long Anglo-French conflict, which, if we confine our attention to the events recorded in the play, has covered a period of about thirty years.[3] His defeat is represented as a symptom of a malady that has atrophied the English war effort, and the disasters in the battlefield are due to the operation and interaction of forces with which Talbot has had nothing to do. There is much greater concentration in the Second Part, in which there are one or two episodes — Jack Cade's rebellion, for example — which are given more importance than is consistent with unity of the plot. The disasters in France are referred to, and they tilt the scales against Suffolk and Somerset, but that is about all there is on the French war. The surrender of Anjou and Maine was part of the marriage contract and belongs really to 1 *Henry VI*. As regards the other possessions, Somerset thus quietly anounces the 'cold news' of their loss:

---

[1] Hall's *Chronicle*, p. 219.
[2] Introduction to 2 *Henry VI* (Imperial Edition).
[3] P. A. Daniel makes it twenty-two years, from the death of Henry V in 1422 to the marriage of Henry VI in 1444 (*Sh. Soc. Trans*, 1879, p. 306). But Talbot died in 1453, and this would make the historic time a little over thirty years.

> all your interest in those territories
> Is utterly bereft you; all is lost.
>
> (III. i. 84–85)

It makes clear that the theme of the Second Part is not foreign war, but civil strife; it is a drama primarily of personal ambition and political intrigue.

As has been pointed out, 2 *Henry VI* divides itself into two halves, each with its own protagonist – the Duke of Gloucester in the first half and the Duke of York in the second. In the first two acts, all the forces combine against Gloucester, and after his death in the Third Act, all that happens in the play converges on a single point – the growing predominance of York. The other characters are intended to play a subordinate role, though sometimes we feel that their importance is either exaggerated, or not properly stressed if the scramble for power is to be correctly grasped. Jack Cade is the most interesting figure in the play, but the space – almost a whole act – given to his adventures is excessive, if we regard York as the protagonist. It is true that York has had something to do with the Kentish rising, but the connexion is so thin that when he returns from Ireland, he does not mention Cade in his soliloquies, and when he gives out that one of the reasons for which he has not disbanded the army is that he wanted to fight the rebel Cade (V. i), no one contradicts the hypocritical plea, though earlier (IV. i) Sir Humphrey Stafford's Brother told Cade that all his pretences were taught by the Duke. It seems that by the time Jack Cade has gained his full stature as a dramatic character, his connexion with the Duke of York's designs on the throne has been forgotten. A different criticism has to be made of the prominence given to the Duke of Somerset in the Fifth Act of 2 *Henry VI*. Till now, although not in the background, he is not one of the major figures in the wranglings portrayed here. But suddenly he becomes the principal target for the Duke of York, who wants to 'heave' him from the Court and the King is anxious to hide him from York. Now Somerset is in the centre of a tense drama, for the Queen clings to him as feverishly as York is determined to throw him out, and it is his head with which the Duke of York's ablest son Richard greets the victorious assembly after the Battle of Saint Alban's, in the opening scene of 3 *Henry VI*. Unless we refer back to the chronicles, there is nothing in the play to prepare us for the pivotal role assigned to Somerset in the closing stages of this play.

This brings us to the principal limitation of a drama (or a novel) that claims to be historical. History is primarily a chronicle of events, and that is why in history as well as in works of art based on history character is often subordinated to action or plot, and the inventive power of the artist partly controlled by recorded facts. If in portraying Cade, the dramatist's imagination has gone beyond the chronicle, he has overstepped the limits of historical drama. Of course, if history objects to such liberty, so much the worse for history! Again, when representing the career of the Duke of York, the dramatist must assign to Somerset the importance he had in history, although it might be out of proportion to the drama as originally conceived. Another weakness stemming from this basic limitation is that history spreads the canvas on which the dramatist or novelist paints his portraits. All historical dramatists (and novelists) – and most of all Shakespeare – have, therefore, to effect a simplification of historical forces and issues in order to be able to focus attention on inner motives and impulses, but as they have to lay emphasis on the movement of events and changes in the background they often miss the subtlety and mystery of human character. This relative superficiality of historical drama will be manifest if we compare the portraits of Humphrey and Eleanor with those of Macbeth and Lady Macbeth. There is similarity in situation and relationship and in both dramas ambitious persons invoke supernatural aid in furtherance of their evil designs. 2 *Henry VI* is an early attempt, and *Macbeth* is one of Shakespeare's noblest achievements; so the comparison here suggested may not be fair to either play. But it gives a tolerably clear idea of the difference between a history play in which the dramatist has to hurry from event to event and a tragedy in which he is free to explore the recesses of character. There are many other instances of this subordination and it is not until we come to *Henry IV* that imagination takes control of fact.

Historical drama selects certain incidents which are often telescoped into one another, and as it cannot go into psychological subtleties characters are portrayed in broad outline rather than in minute detail. This simplification is suitable for didactic treatment, and we may be tempted to look upon Elizabethan historical drama as an extension of the methods and principles of the morality play out of which it grew. The semi-historical plays before Shakespeare, such as *The Misfortunes of King Arthur* and *King Cambyses* were moralities, and there is a strong moralistic strain in such Chronicle plays as *The Famous Victories of Henry the Fifth*, *The Troublesome Raigne of King John*, and *The True Tragedie of Richard the third*, which possibly served as sources and models for Shakespeare. How far Shakespeare's work in historical drama is amenable to such an interpretation has already been discussed in some detail, but the question has to be re-examined in a study of 2 *Henry VI*, which seems especially designed to enforce a moral lesson. The chronicler Hall, who was Shakespeare's ultimate authority, was anti-Beaufort; he draws a very dark picture of the Cardinal of Winchester and presents his enemy, the Protector, as the 'good Duke Humphrey'. But being a historian, Hall is not blind to the Protector's frailties, particularly his weakness for women – his questionable relations with Jacqueline of Hainault, whom he stole from her first husband, and with Eleanor Cobham, who was first his 'soveraigne lady and paramour' and then his wife. And Hall concedes, too, that the Cardinal of Winchester was 'a great stay to the Kyng and the realme', and that after his death, 'the affayres in France, were neither well looked to, nor the governors of the countrey were well advised'.[1] In his taste for simplification Shakespeare passes over Gloucester's faults and makes no reference to Winchester's virtues. The affair of Jacqueline is nowhere mentioned, and there is nothing disgraceful in the Protector's relations with Eleanor Cobham, his ambitious wife. On the other hand, Winchester is represented even in the first scene of 1 *Henry VI* as a Machiavellian priest who does not want to remain long a Jack out of office, and later on emphasis is placed only on his pride and his unscrupulous ambition. Moreover, in Shakespeare's drama he is directly implicated in the murder of the Duke of Gloucester, and he dies of remorse immediately after this heinous crime. From the chronicle account we know that Winchester died quite a few weeks after the murder of Gloucester, with which he seems to have had nothing to do, and his death-bed delirium, as reported by Hall, makes no reference to this crime. It is Shakespeare who makes the delirium colourful by inserting into it a tortured confession of guilt for Gloucester's murder:

> Bring me unto my trial when you will.
> Died he not in his bed? Where should he die?
> Can I make men live whe'r they will or no?

---

[1] Hall's *Chronicle*, p. 211.

O! torture me no more, I will confess.
Alive again? then show me where he is:
I'll give a thousand pound to look upon him.
He hath no eyes, the dust hath blinded them.
Comb down his hair; look! look! it stands upright,
Like lime-twigs set to catch my winged soul.
Give me some drink; and bid the apothecary
Bring the strong poison that I bought of him.

(III. iii. 8–18)

The first half of 2 *Henry VI* looks, indeed, like a morality play on honest statesmanship set off against unscrupulous ambition. Although Good is sacrificed, Evil does not thrive. The punishment of Winchester and Suffolk is swift – in history there is an interval of three years between Winchester's death and Suffolk's banishment – and that of Margaret is delayed till towards the end of this play and beyond this play to its successor. J. P. Brockbank looks upon 2 *Henry VI* as a morality on the sacrifice of Gloucester and the consequent dissolution of law; he observes in its central acts 'the confluence of the Senecal dramatic tradition, with its ruthless retributive morality, and the Christian (or Hebraic) cult of *Vindicta Dei*'[1]. Tillyard, who recognizes the firmer dramatic treatment of materials in the Second Part of *Henry VI* as contrasted with the First, stresses what he considers the essentially didactic nature of the play. The large variety of incidents and characters shows that not merely the nobility but the whole frame of *Respublica* is in agony. In the political chaos unleashed by the ambitious barons, Alexander Iden stands apart as the 'symbol of degree', a dimmer counterpart of the majestic Talbot of the First Part. According to Tillyard, Iden indicates the design of the play when he says that he does not seek 'to wax great by others' waning'. That is the ungenerous aim of the majority of the nobles – most offensively, of 'dogged York, that reaches at the moon'. On this view, the play may also be taken as an enquiry into the nature of kingship, for there are three regal figures in the forefront – King Henry, Gloucester, and York, and all of them are unfit to rule. Henry has the nature of a pelican but not of a lion or a fox; Gloucester is a pelican and a lion, not a fox; and York a lion and a fox but not a pelican.[2] Wilson Knight finds a basic sense of moral law in pious Henry's oft-quoted exclamation:[3]

[1] *Early Shakespeare*, p. 86.
[2] *Shakespeare's History Plays*, pp. 174–86.
[3] *The Sovereign Flower*, p. 14.

What stronger breastplate than a heart untainted!
Thrice is he arm'd that hath his quarrel just,
And he but naked, though lock'd up in steel,
Whose conscience with injustice is corrupted.

(III. ii. 232–5)

For Reese the central figure is York, and 2 *Henry VI* 'adopts in the main the structure of the morality, with *Respublica* threatened by the various personifications of Lust, Pride and Ambition; and the special political lesson that Shakespeare wishes to use for the instruction of his contemporaries is that prescriptive right – York has a better claim to the throne than Henry, – does not justify an attack on the *de facto* possessor'.[1]

If we confine our attention to the play itself, it will be seen that there is little justification for reading it as a morality, for not one of the above theories emerges out of the interaction between plot and character, in which lies the substance of Shakespearian drama. Henry claims that there is no stronger breastplate than a heart untainted and that a man who has a just quarrel is thrice armed, but although Henry has an untainted heart, is his quarrel just? All through this play and also in the other plays in which this question is raised, it is clearly suggested that the Lancastrian title is weak and Henry himself, although somewhat falteringly, recognizes this. But there is not a scrap of evidence to suggest that rebellion, even for a right cause, is unjustified. This problem is raised in *King John*, where different characters approach it in different ways, but not in this play where might fights with might. Indeed, the three parts of *Henry VI* are the nearest approach to perfect amoral history: Henry has an untainted heart and York has a just quarrel, but both come to grief. Nor can we say that Shakespeare juxtaposes different specimens of royalty in order to develop his own view of a perfect king. There is no doubt that Henry is a very pious man and yet unfit to occupy the throne at a time when the king must either rule or be ruled. On the other hand, York's strength and craftiness are never presented as virtues that Henry VI would have done well to imitate. The good Duke Humphrey is outnumbered and outmanoeuvred by unscrupulous adventurers and let down by his wife's guilty ambition. The first half of 2 *Henry VI* has the appearance of a morality, but the simple morality structure is complicated by Eleanor Cobham's arrogance and treasonable designs. Departing from history where

[1] *The Cease of Majesty*, p. 181.

Eleanor was disgraced long before Margaret's marriage, Shakespeare brings the two ambitious women together and the drama becomes too personal and complex to fit into any narrow pattern. Eleanor's ambition provides Margaret and her accomplices with an excuse for their campaign against Gloucester, who becomes tainted with his wife's criminal folly which he cannot stop and does not expose, and no simple generalization can be made out of this tense drama of intricate personal rivalry. If, as many Tudor moralists have argued, Henry VI suffered for his grandfather's crime, how much more contaminated must Gloucester be by his wife's unlawful ambition? Shakespeare tells the same story we find in his sources and analogues, but while making it more vivid and endowing the wooden figures of history with 'an active life', he does not bring out the moral so facilely drawn by his Elizabethan contemporaries or his modern critics.

In his earliest plays as well as in his latest, Shakespeare takes a total view of life and although the total view includes the moralistic interpretation it also transcends it. Indeed, a proper appreciation of Shakespeare's plays shows how drama emerges out of the narrow structure of the morality, and the most important feature of 2 *Henry VI* is that it reveals a large area of life, sweeping forward in continuous movement. In spite of the fact that in this play there is no French scene and all the incidents take place in England, there is much greater variety than in the First Part, for characters are taken from all walks of life. There are noblemen and ordinary men, hardy soldiers as well as hardened sea-dogs, high-born lords and ladies as well as disreputable conjurors and ragamuffins and impostors. Jack Cade and his associates are given more space than their rebellion may rightfully claim in a historical play, and the Simpcox incident violates the canon of unity, because its removal will not 'disjoin and dislocate the whole'. But even the characters that lie on the fringe of the action and the incidents that are loosely connected contribute to the impression of comprehensiveness. It is a large world that has been set in motion by the warring ambitions of the lords and ladies of the Court, in whom there is greater complexity than in the monolithic figures of the First Part. Not that there is, except in Jack Cade, any trace of the intricate artistry we find in Shakespeare's greater dramas, but there are some indications of his later workmanship. Gloucester is a good steward of the realm, but neither his clinging to office nor his wrangling with Winchester is pelican-like. Margaret makes an uneasy compromise between devotion to a lover and fidelity to her husband, and more compelling than either of these traits is her lust for power. York has a passionate sense of the injustice done to his family, but he is also a Machiavellian intriguer and a violent disrupter of public tranquillity. Jack Cade, the most subtly drawn character in the whole play, is a complex figure who combines a soaring imagination with a hard sense of reality, and wants to establish a commonwealth in which the most uncompromising despotism is compatible with the most broad-based democracy.

This play produces another impression that is dramatically more suggestive. It not only presents a large area of life but presents it as in continuous progress. This is different from the flux presented in the First Part, where the same kind of change – victory followed by defeat – is noticeable from one stage of the action to another. Indeed, there seems to be no adequate reason – in spite of the defeat and death of Talbot, which is followed immediately by the capture of Joan – why the English should be anxious for peace, and the proposal of marriage between King Henry and Margaret of Anjou is more the result of a personal fascination than a military or diplomatic necessity. 2 *Henry VI* is dynamic in a different way; here the movement is not wheel-like but wavy and winding. The squabbles which at the beginning were purely personal have now acquired a broader basis, because Winchester, the principal enemy of Gloucester, has been strengthened by the support of the Queen and her paramour Suffolk, and they proceed to throw the Protector out. York is interested in Gloucester's disgrace and death, but he stands aloof, and two of the Yorkists – Salisbury and Warwick – seem to be puzzled. Although adherents of the Yorkist cause, they appreciate the services rendered by Gloucester and are interested in the welfare of the commonwealth:

> Join we together for the public good,
> In what we can to bridle and suppress
> The pride of Suffolk and the cardinal,
> With Somerset's and Buckingham's ambition;
> And, as we may, cherish Duke Humphrey's deeds,
> While they do tend the profit of the land.
>
> (I. i. 200–05)

But they can do little to protect the good Duke from his enemies and do not bestir themselves until it is too late. There is another quarrel – equally personal – between York and Somerset, and the Queen tries to smooth it over by cajoling both the contestants. But after Gloucester's death in mysterious circumstances, there is a fresh alignment of forces, and purely personal bickerings now quicken into rivalry for the throne. Beaufort dies from remorse, and Suffolk is banished, never to return. At the end of his Irish expedition York comes back and not only demands the removal of Somerset, who, he says, rules the roast in governmental affairs, but openly challenges Henry's right to occupy the throne:

> Here is a hand to hold a sceptre up,
> And with the same to act controlling laws.
> Give place: by heaven, thou shalt rule no more
> O'er him whom heaven created for thy ruler.
>
> (V. i. 102–05)

On the eve of his Irish assignment, Queen Margaret addressed him as 'good York' and seemed to hope that she would be able to smother the 'raging fire' between him and Somerset. But soon she finds that she only helped – in York's own words – to 'warm the starving snake'. Court intrigue now broadens into a civil war, which, drawing a sharp line of distinction between the two Roses, spreads beyond the confines of the Court to the wider public. Salisbury and Warwick, as champions of the commons, succeed in getting Suffolk banished, and they now openly denounce the King and espouse the White Rose. The Red Rose finds a doughty champion in Clifford and the civil war is in full tide. Here we have the 'confusion', of which the Duke of Exeter spoke in 1 *Henry IV* (IV. i), and the 'jarring discord of nobility' is having a larger impact than even the principal actors can foresee.

From yet another point of view there is an impression of progressive movement in this play such as we do not find in the First Part of the trilogy. In 1 *Henry VI*, Salisbury and Bedford die old, and Talbot's age is set off against his son's youth, but there is no impression of one generation handing over the torch of life to another. The advent in the Fifth Act of Suffolk and Margaret, who look forward to the future, seems to be an abrupt transition. But it is such transition from the old generation to the new that is strikingly expressed in 2 *Henry VI*. York begins taking over in devious ways the reins of power once held by Gloucester, and in spite of the carnage that has been let loose we feel that a hardy warrior and crafty diplomat is supplanting a man of ebbing energy, who, even before he is murdered, has become a back-number. Behind the ageing, though still vigorous York, loom his two sons – Edward, and even more than Edward, Richard, whose words and deeds give unmistakable indication of the sweeping changes that will soon follow. Old Clifford is militant and murderous, but he dies, leaving his more brutal son to carry on the remorseless vendetta. We find a similar difference if we look at the progress of the Nevils – father and son. At first, both of them – Salisbury and Warwick – were half-indifferent spectators in the quest for power, the father slightly more important than the son. But Salisbury speaks eloquently of the potential might of the latter:

> Thy deeds, thy plainness, and thy house-keeping,
> Have won the greatest favour of the commons,
> Excepting none but good Duke Humphrey:
>
> (I. i. 192–4)

and before long as the main pillar of the Yorkist cause, Warwick flings defiance at Clifford:

> This day I will wear aloft my burgonet, –
> As on a mountain-top the cedar shows,
> That keeps his leaves in spite of any storm, –
> Even to affright thee with the view thereof.
>
> (V. i. 204–07)

In the final assault on Saint Alban's, although York pays due honour to Salisbury,

> That winter lion, who in rage forgets
> Aged contusions and all brush of time,
>
> (V. iii. 2–3)

it is the son Warwick who has come definitely to the forefront, and the last lines in the fifth Act are spoken by this sturdy warrior and diplomat, who in the next play will make and un-make kings.

IV

'The third part of Henry VI', says Tillyard, 'is Shakespeare's nearest approach to the Chronicle play'.[1] And the opinion is largely true. In this play, as also in the First Part, he draws on a vast body of chronicle material, but here although he takes liberties, he treats his materials with fidelity, bringing out their

---

[1] *Shakespeare's History Plays*, p. 190.

'accidental (and partly chronological) relations'. The thrilling events constituting the plot come in close succession and are grouped round certain characters – Henry and Margaret on the one side and York and Edward on the other. With the exception of Henry VI who contrasts sharply with the society he moves in, all the important figures are governed by lust for power and thirst for vengeance. We seldom see behind the surface into those instincts and elementary inhibitions in which lies the essence of personality; even Richard of Gloucester, the most powerfully drawn figure in the play, seems to hide himself behind a mask. Tillyard holds that while writing this play Shakespeare was 'tired' and 'bored',[1] and he detects a certain falling-off from the standard reached in the Second Part. This, however, does less than justice to the play's dramatic vividness and Shakespeare's capacity for organizing a mass of materials. No episode is given undue prominence here and no episode hangs loosely from the dramatic fabric; from this point of view there is an improvement on rather than a falling-off from Part Two. The historical period covered by the plot of 3 *Henry VI* is the span of twenty years from the First Battle of Saint Alban's (1455) to the ransoming of Margaret (1475), and the time represented on the stage is, according to Daniel, as many days.[2] The various episodes of the plot are so intimately connected that the action progresses in a continuous line without a jolt and without a diversion. There is a central theme – the supersession of the Red Rose by the White – and one episode so smoothly slides into another that there is no break when Edward takes up the Yorkist leadership from his father. Richard, York's youngest son, about whom more will have to be said presently, stands out, without any basis in history, as the most prominent character, but even he is only a part of the crowded stage, and it is not till the end, when we are on the threshold of the next play, that we have the first glimpse of his loneliness.

The impression produced by 3 *Henry VI* is of a grand procession rather than of the dramatic interaction of plot and character. Events separated by many years are telescoped, irrelevant details are rejected and new episodes added – all with a view to producing an impression of vivid contrast. The chronicles dwell emphatically on the ever-changing tide of Fortune, and Shakespeare gives a

---

[1] ibid., 198.
[2] P. A. Daniel, *Time-analysis of the Plots of Shakespeare's Plays* (Sh. Soc. Trans., 1879), p. 324.

graphic account of this fluctuation through characterization, imagery, and primarily through the organization of plot. An analysis of a few striking scenes will reveal how Shakespeare's genius explores and utilizes the dramatic possibilities of the chronicle narrative. The first scene covers a period of five years from 1455 to York's openly claiming the throne in 1460. Here a relatively small skirmish at Northampton (1459) is merged with the more decisive battle at Saint Alban's (1455), after which the Queen took five long years to muster an army and oppose the Yorkists at Wakefield (1460). In history, King Henry VI escaped arrest in the Battle of Saint Alban's but was taken captive at Northampton, after which York boldly proceeded to occupy the throne. In the drama, York's public assertion of his claim to the throne is not without an element of irony. It was the King – or rather the Queen – who called the Parliament, but before the Queen can gather her forces, York, with the assistance of the intrepid Warwick, becomes master of an assembly convened by his enemies. His assumption of royalty, both sudden and pre-meditated, has its different stages, one dramatically following another. First, there is an account of the almost total eclipse of the Lancastrian cause, and when Richard throws down the head of Somerset, York's 'dearest foe', as a natural climax, Warwick raises York to the 'regal seat', proclaiming boldly:

> Resolve thee, Richard; claim the English crown.
>
> (I. i. 49)

His speech is scarcely ended when enters King Henry with his straggling followers and there is a slanging match between the supporters of the rival claimants to the throne. In history, a compromise, allowing Henry to rule for his lifetime, was forced on the Yorkists by the Parliament. But Shakespeare makes Henry appeal to the Yorkists to allow him to reign for as long as he lives, his weakness furnishing a pitiful contrast to the haughty spirit of his enemy, who swooped upon his throne like 'an empty eagle', as also of his own champion, the formidable Lord Clifford. Just then, once again in partial defiance of history, Margaret breaks in upon the Parliament and scatters the compromise to the winds. Here there is wave-like movement, and the end of the scene leaves the audience in tense expectation of what is to come next.

The second scene takes us to the Battle of Wakefield, in which the Yorkists are routed and the Duke of York is slain. In representing this Yorkist defeat, Shakespeare follows history in the main but also makes a few significant changes which transform the bloody engagement into a lurid dramatic spectacle. He omits the part of Sir Davy Halle, York's 'old servaunt and chief counsailer', who dissuaded him from giving battle until re-inforced by his son Edward, who was expected to come with his power of Marchmen and Welsh soldiers. In Shakespeare's version, not only is the Earl of March present in the Battle of Wakefield, but he and his younger brother Richard encourage their father to break his oath to the Lancastrians and to 'bid them battle straight'. Passing over the Rutland episode (I. iii), which is very much on the lines of the chronicle narrative, we may proceed to a consideration of the next scene which has become memorable on account of Greene's parodying one of its lines. The most spectacular incident in this long scene representing the defeat and death of the Duke of York is based on a very brief and prosaic account in Hall's *Chronicle*:

'Yet this cruell Clifforde, & deadly bloudsupper not content with this homicyde, or chyldkillyng, came to the place wher the dead corps of the duke of Yorke lay, and caused his head to be stryken of, and set on it a croune of paper, & so fixed it on a pole, & presented it to the Queene, not lyeng farre from the felde, in great despite, and much derision. . . . After this victory by the Quene and her parte obteyned, she caused the erle of Salisbury, with all the other prisoners, to bee sente to Pomfret, and there to bee behedded, and sent all their heddes, and the dukes head of Yorke, to be set upon poles, over the gate of the citie of Yorke . . .'[1]

In Shakespeare's drama, York is captured alive and delivered to Margaret, who is present on the battlefield – 'A woman's general', York's son Richard commented derisively – and then Margaret makes him sit on a molehill before putting a paper crown on his head, thus mocking his aspirations and parodying the opening scene of the play, in which with Warwick's assistance he did possess the regal seat. It is in this way that Hall's description comes to life, and at the apex of her power Margaret glares terrifically as the 'She-wolf of France'. The long drawn out recrimination between York and Margaret has a touch of bombast; it holds the action in suspense, but it is full of vitality and vigour. It is dramatically appropriate that the idea of putting a paper crown on York's head occurs to Margaret, the principal agent of the Lancastrian cause, and herself a queen, rather than to Clifford,

[1] p. 251.

who however brutal and remorseless, was only one of her instruments.

A word may be said of the deft manner in which Shakespeare quickens the pace of action and yet marks intervals of time. In history there was a gap of several months between the Battle of Wakefield, where the Duke of York was defeated and killed and the Battle of Towton, where the Lancastrians were routed and Edward was able to proclaim himself king. In the interval between these two major engagements, Warwick, the pillar of the Yorkist cause, suffered a reverse in what is known as the second battle of Saint Alban's, but a few weeks before Towton, far away in the West, Edward was victorious at the battle of Mortimer's Cross. The Folio does not mark any division into acts and scenes, but modern editors rightly close the First Act with York's death at Wakefield. When Edward hears of it and is joined by Warwick, we are told that at least ten days have passed since the catastrophe, and Warwick's defeat in the interval, made vivid by Richard's sardonic comments here and Margaret's sarcasm later on, is merely reported. The action moves from Wakefield to Towton with breathless speed, and yet there is an impression of orderly progress from defeat to recovery. H. C. Hart complains that there is much confusion here, because Edward was in Gloucester when he heard of his father's death and there is no room in the drama for the battle of Mortimer's Cross which was fought quite a long time after.[1] But such a view does not take note of the difference between history which records the progress of events in strict chronological succession and historical drama which imposes its own order on the mass of materials provided by history. Shakespeare directly represents only the decisive battles – Wakefield, Towton, and later on, Barnet. The other battles are dexterously interwoven into the main story. The second battle of Saint Alban's is graphically reported; the engagement at Mortimer's Cross, which seems to be both a part of and a sequel to Wakefield, is made memorable by the reference to the strange phenomenon of three suns, which occurred at about this time; and Barnet runs into Tewksbury, which dealt a death-blow to the Lancastrian cause. Shakespeare's dramatic art condenses and invigorates the historical narrative, correctly representing the ebb and flow in the tide of Fortune. Although one battle is telescoped into another and gaps between successive incidents are

---

[1] Notes in the Arden Shakespeare, p. 38.

sometimes ignored, there is no confusion in the narrative. It gives intact the substance of history, even if a few details become obscure in the process of dramatic transformation.

There is another memorable scene (III. iii), in which compression results in vivid contrast, though some critics have objected to the way in which Shakespeare, while maintaining dramatic sequence, connects widely separated incidents. Queen Margaret, who sought the assistance of the French King, and Warwick, who canvassed a diplomatic marriage for Edward with a French Princess, did not visit the French court on the same day though both of them went to France at about the same time (1464); and although Warwick had been nursing his grievances against Edward IV for a long while, he did not go over to the Lancastrians until 1470. Shakespeare compresses the events of several years into a single episode, in which the King of France promises aid to Margaret, is tempted by Warwick's bribe to abandon her, and then finally vows a crusade against Edward. Not only is this swift change of alliance spectacular but it also gives a vivid idea of late medieval society, in which a vassal baron is fiercely devoted to his king but, being a semi-independent master of fiefs, can also challenge his authority and readily exchange one loyalty for another. Not that Warwick is a subtly drawn character. Indeed, the play itself does not furnish adequate evidence to show how he came to be a king-maker. Here history gives us a mass of information about his position and character, and Shakespeare has failed properly to dramatize it. But his career – with its shifting loyalties between Humphrey and York and then from Edward IV to Henry VI – is characteristic of an age in which every moral principle was sacrificed to the lust for power.

3 *Henry VI* is a chronicle account rather than a historical play, because both in narration and characterization it follows, with one exception, the lines laid down by Hall and others. That one exception is Richard of Gloucester, the Duke of York's youngest son, whom Shakespeare deliberately gives a prominence that is flatly contradicted by facts. In 2 *Henry VI*, he plays an important part in the Battle of Saint Alban's, killing Somerset, but at the time of this battle he was a toddler of three, and he could not have been present at Wakefield, where his father died in an unequal conflict; he was then seven years old and soon away from England. 'The duches of Yorke', says Hall, 'seyng her husband and sonne slayne, and not knowyng what should succede of her eldest

sonnes chaunces, sent her. ii. younger sonnes, George & Richard, over the sea, to the citie of Wtrechte in Almayn: where they were of Philippe, duke of Bourgoyne, well receyved and fested, and so there thei remayned, till their brother Edwarde had obteyned the Realme, and gotten the regiment. . . .'[1] Shakespeare ignores this clear direction of history and gives him a prominence that at this stage did not belong to him. Indeed, it is for his sake that Shakespeare minimizes the importance of his eldest brother who played a leading part in the events dramatized in 3 *Henry VI*, and later on he passes quickly over what Hall calls the prosperous reign of Edward IV. Shakespeare must have given excessive importance to Richard designedly, and the design is primarily aesthetic and only incidentally moral. The Wars of the Roses appeared to his Tudor imagination as a clash of rival ambitions which made light of moral scruples. Richard is the latest of the agents in this holocaust, and he is in every sense the greatest of them all. He has all the brutality and greed for power seen in Clifford, Margaret, and Warwick and yet a zestfulness combined with a sardonic humour which sets him above them. In him unprincipled ambition reaches its climax and with him it comes to an appropriate end. Whether Henry VI or the Duke of York had the better title to the throne or whether the rebellion of Bolingbroke in the past or that of the Yorkists later on is justified is a politico-ethical problem which Shakespeare leaves unresolved. But there is no doubt that Richard of Gloucester, the youngest of the Duke of York's sons, had not originally even a shadow of a claim; in Shakespeare's play, however, he is determined, quite early in life, to sweep his way to the throne, because he lives in a world where it is an accepted principle that Providence is on the stronger side, and where none but the impotent Henry VI makes 'weapons' of 'holy saws of sacred writ'. Indeed, in this 'miserable age', success is the only criterion by which one is to judge whether a thing is good or bad. The Father who has unknowingly killed his Son exclaims in horror:

> What stratagems, how fell, how butcherly,
> Erroneous, mutinous, and unnatural,
> This deadly quarrel daily doth beget!
>
> (II. v. 89–91)

All that is 'butcherly, erroneous, mutinous and unnatural' is symbolized in this one figure. Even his shape is unnatural. Young

---

[1] Hall's *Chronicle*, p. 253.

Clifford addresses him as 'Foul indigested lump', and Henry VI details the many evil signs that at the time of his birth foreboded a luckless time. He takes all these allegations in good humour, for he finds in them an anticipation of his later career and a justification for his murderous Machiavellism:

> I came into the world with my legs forward.
> Had I not reason, think ye, to make haste,
> And seek their ruin that usurp'd our right?
>
> * * *
>
> Then, since the heavens have shaped my body so,
> Let hell make crook'd my mind to answer it.
>
> (V. vi. 71 ff.)

In the above lines he speaks of 'our right', meaning the right of his family. But even from the beginning he has no loyalty, no real consideration for the interests of others. In a world dominated by greed for power, he is the perfect egoist; he is himself alone. In him we see the fulfilment of the principles or the lack of any principle that guided the barons who took part in the Wars of the Roses.

It has been pointed out above that he has the dauntless, reckless brutality that we find in a smaller measure in the other leading figures, but not in Henry VI after whom the trilogy is named, who is a pious man, and unfit, partly because of this very piety, to control his unruly barons. Richard is not unaware of piety, but he knows it only for purposes of mockery and parody. He wants to send Young Clifford to sup in heaven with Jesus, and if Clifford objects he will be accommodated as readily in the other place. At his birth, the women discovered to their horror that he had already his teeth, and they cried in dismay, 'O! Jesus bless us'; he would say 'amen' to this, for it signifies Heaven's intention to make of him a snarling, biting dog. He makes a division of labour between priests and princes: while the former pray, the latter kill, and he himself wants to tell his devotion with revengeful arms on the helmets of his foes. He stabs Henry VI dead in the penultimate scene of this play, and later on justifies this heinous act on the plea that he only helped to send the holy saint to heaven!

Both in theory and practice Richard is an exponent of what later came to be popularly described as Machiavellism; and Henry VI, a man of church-like humours and bookish rule, enunciates a philosophy of pastoral content, far from the madding barons' ferocious strife. That is why critics with a didactic turn have been tempted to look upon this play as primarily a clash between these two protagonists. According to Reese, 'the play's interest is withdrawn from the lesser men and their predestined doings and is concentrated upon the two who stand at opposite extremes of good and evil. Henry lacks the power of action, but his saintliness and serenity shed their own illumination; Richard, the man of deeds, is sheerly wicked. The play moves to its climax under the shadow of their conflict'.[1] Henry VI does not play any important part in the trilogy of which he is the titular hero, but he is the central character because all the incidents revolve round him, and he is a contrast to the other figures because he is a good man without ambition and they are ferociously ambitious people without goodness. He is a saintly man and yet very much a man. He is open to the charm of beauty, even on hearsay; that is the only explanation for his accepting the bride chosen by Suffolk. Although unfit for the office of a king, he yet clings to the throne and is even ready to disinherit his son if he is allowed to reign during his lifetime. But in his heart of hearts he loves the Glad Poverty held forth as an ideal by Boccaccio and Lydgate, whereas the powerful people about him are imbued with the Renaissance lust for power. In a sense he stands severely alone, but in his holiness and helplessness he is a refreshing contrast to his sordid environment. This contrast, suggested all through the play, reaches its climax in the last scene but one where the pious man, sitting at his book, is set upon and stabbed to death by his most brutal enemy.

Although Henry VI is the nominal hero, Richard is the most dominant actor in the drama of the Wars of the Roses as presented by Shakespeare. Indeed, the tetralogy seems to move to a climax only as the other characters recede into the background, and the threads of the action are gathered together in his hands. In 3 *Henry VI*, he appears in nineteen of its twenty-eight scenes and Henry only in seven. As the play opens and the lords begin to give an account of their exploits, with a touch of theatricality – he will make fine art of it later on – Richard throws down the head of Somerset to speak for him. In the next scene, he takes the initiative in persuading his father to break his oath of allegiance to King Henry. Here he reveals another characteristic trait – his command

---

[1] *The Cease of Majesty*, p. 205.

of sophisticated reasoning – of wrenching the wrong cause to make it look right. One of the off-shoots of his soaring ambition and self-confidence is his contempt for his enemy, and this proves to be a false guide now. The Duke of York would have braved the Lancastrian forces even if he had not been there to encourage the desperate move. But Richard's scornful attitude is characteristic, and his father pays dearly for it as he himself will do later. In defeat and disaster he does not lose heart; tears are for babes and blows and revenge for him, and it is in this spirit that he puts courage into the heart of his eldest brother who seems to be unmanned by their father's death. But his intellect is never clouded by his emotions; he mildly taunts Warwick for his flight and quibbles on Edward's weakness for 'breeders'. At the Battle of Towton, although the leadership belongs nominally to Edward, he is easily the most distinguished and self-possessed soldier. It is he who takes the leading part in rescuing Edward from captivity, but as soon as the Yorkists are triumphant and the Red Rose is crushed, his monstrosity is revealed in its true colours. So far he has been the most valiant champion of the cause of his father and brother, but now he stands alone in his egoism – the scourge of the White Rose as previously he was of the Red. The Wars of the Roses come to an end after throwing their most terrible progeny to the fore-front, and there is pathetic irony in the self-complacent speech with which King Edward closes this part of the tetralogy:

> And now what rests but that we spend the time
> With stately triumphs, mirthful comic shows,
> Such as befit the pleasure of the court?
> Sound, drums and trumpets! farewell, sour annoy!
> For here, I hope, begins our lasting joy.
>
> (V. vii. 42–46)

How short-lived this 'lasting joy' is will appear in the final play of this series.

V

Richard III is Shakespeare's first attempt at making a tragedy out of a chronicle theme. Shakespeare's 'histories' depict generally a long period of time in which there is a multiplicity of incidents and more than one protagonist dominates the stage. Tragedy, however, demands much greater cohesion than is possible in a

sprawling narrative with a profusion of both incidents and characters. Aeschylus in the *Persae* solved this problem in a manner
consonant with the conventions of the Athenian theatre. It has
been said that in a sense all the dramas written by Aeschylus,
Sophocles and Euripides are historical, because all of them are
based on legends that were once believed to be true. But the
Persae is different from the other Greek tragedies that have come
down to us, for it takes an incident from the recent past about
which there was greater certitude than about the far-off matter
of Troy or of Thebes. And Aeschylus succeeds in giving here
greater details of past incidents, both about the enormous Persian
preparation and the smashing defeat, than we find in his own
Oresteia or the *Oedipus Tyrannus* of Sophocles. Yet Aeschylus is not
interested in describing the various episodes in the great naval
battle which is the theme of his tragedy or the part played by the
leaders assembled on either side. He fixes his attention on one
particular point in the story, and inserts as many names or touches
on as many episodes as may be consistent with his concentration
on this supreme moment of defeat. In a sense, the *Persae* has no
plot, and whatever characterization it has – the plot requires no
more than two actors besides the chorus – is broad and vague.
The details are indistinct, but such indistinctness is not an
artistic blemish, because it helps to enforce a single, overwhelming
impression.

Shakespeare's attitude seems to have been different. He took
long periods of history, covering, except in *Richard II*, many
years with a large number of incidents and characters, and the
impression produced by his plays is one of largeness, of expansiveness both in space and time. In *Richard III* and partly also in 3
Henry VI, however, he tries to give cohesion to this multifarious-
ness by directing attention to one prominent person who dominates the scene. In Shakespeare's workshop these two plays show
how tragedy as an art-form emerges out of the profusion of
historical materials. The incidents in these two plays cluster
round one central figure – the Duke of York's youngest son,
Richard of Gloucester, who is introduced in 2 *Henry VI* in defiance
of history, and who, once again without historical warrant,
comes gradually to occupy the leading position in 3 *Henry VI*. In
the play which bears his own name, although history is more
faithfully followed than in the other plays of the tetralogy, it is
his dominating personality rather than the events he dominates

which is the centre of dramatic interest. Aristotle deprecates the
unity that is derived from making the life of one man the subject
of tragedy, for an infinity of things may befall the one man and
it may not be possible to reduce them to unity.[1] Shakespeare does
not seek unity through one man but through one character, that is
to say, he omits many incidents that happened to the historical
Richard and adds one or two – the wooing of Anne, for example –
which are imaginary, but only such incidents are reproduced from
history or invented by the dramatist as reveal the character of the
protagonist.

Clarence is the most enigmatic figure in the two final plays in
the tetralogy; in the chronicles neither his defection from
Warwick nor his death is sufficiently motivated or explained.
Already in 3 *Henry VI*, Shakespeare is primarily interested in
Richard and matters not directly concerned with him are relegated
to the background. That Edward IV and Clarence fell out and that
Clarence was by the King's order done to death is correct history,
but even sixteenth century historians could not say anything very
precise about the cause of the quarrel between the two brothers.
According to Polydore Vergil, who is not quite sure about his
information, there was serious disagreement between the King
and Clarence, because the latter wanted to marry the only daughter
of the Duke of Burgundy – his first wife, Warwick's daughter
must have been dead by then – and the King, envying his brother's
prosperity, 'hinderyd that affynytie'; Clarence also vehemently
protested against the execution of one of his servants by the order
of the King, and there was a foolish prophecy that Edward IV
would be succeeded by one the first letter of whose name should
be G.[2] More, whom both Hall and Holinshed follow, is equally
uncertain:

'. . . were it by the quene or nobles of her blud, whiche highly
maligned the kynges kynred . . . or wer it a proud appetite of the duke
hym selfe, entendynge to bee kynge, at the leaste wise, heinous treason
was laied to his charge, and finally were he in faulte or wer he faultlesse,
attainted was he by parliament and judged to death, and there upon
hastely drowned in a batte of malmsey within the toure of London'.

More further refers to a surmise made by wise men that Richard,
Duke of Gloucester, helped forth Clarence to his death, though
all the while pretending solicitude for him. But in all these matters

---

[1] *On the Art of Poetry*, pp. 41–42.
[2] *Three Books of Polydore Vergil's English History*, pp. 167–8.

More feels that he is on uncertain ground, and 'whosoever divineth upon conjectures maie as well shote to fer as to short'.[1]

In Shakespeare's version, there is reference to Clarence's disaffection on account of the King's bestowal of eligible brides on his wife's relations instead of on his brothers. That is why he plays the broker in his own behalf and proceeds to marry Warwick's younger daughter, the elder having been already affianced to King Henry VI's son. This is the explanation for a minor departure from history where the younger daughter is bethrothed to the Prince, because the elder was, at the time of the betrothal, wife of Clarence. Dramatically, the change is an improvement, because it emphasizes quite early the rift between the Queen's party and the King's brothers and makes it possible for the dramatist to ignore the other causes of the first estrangement between Clarence and Edward. But the modification is not without its disadvantage, too, for it prevents Shakespeare from adequately motivating Clarence's desertion of Warwick. In *Richard III*, Shakespeare, following the *Mirror for Magistrates*, passes over the many speculations made by Polydore Vergil and others about the possible causes of Clarence's incarceration and death; in his account there is nothing vague or uncertain about this puzzling move, for it was brought about by the machinations of his brother, the Duke of Gloucester, who says:

> Plots have I laid, inductions dangerous,
> By drunken prophecies, libels, and dreams,
> To set my brother Clarence and the king
> In deadly hate the one against the other:
> And if King Edward be as true and just
> As I am subtle, false, and treacherous,
> This day should Clarence closely be mew'd up,
> About a prophecy, which says that G
> Of Edward's heirs the murderer shall be.
>
> (*Richard III*, I. i. 32–40)

So far we have seen Richard as a remorseless but extremely capable soldier, and now he emerges as a crafty manipulator of men and women. With slight hints from history, Shakespeare makes him attempt impossible tasks, which however fantastic to others, appear to be a walk-over for him. The King, the lords around him, Clarence himself and the Queen who is supposed to

---

[1] Hall's *Chronicle*, pp. 342–3.

be hostile to Clarence – all seem to be hypnotized into imbecility. More speaks of the haste with which Clarence was done to death, and this small suggestion is worked into a dramatic announcement of the deed. Ironically enough, at a meeting of reconciliation during the King's last illness – in history Clarence pre-deceased his brother by five years – it is the Queen who urges her husband to take Clarence to his grace, whereupon she is thus sharply rebuked by Richard:

> Why, madam, have I offer'd love for this,
> To be so flouted in this royal presence?
> Who knows not that the gentle duke is dead?
> [*They all start.*]
>
> (II. i. 78–80)

The dying King exclaims in helpless agony: 'Who knows not he is dead! Who knows he is?' He countermanded the earlier order of execution, but the swiftest messenger would be too slow for Richard's devilry.

Shakespeare's account of the Clarence story is fantastic and may not be in itself credible, for he does not reveal the plots and inductions dangerous by means of which Richard accomplishes his fell purpose. But his account of the way in which he has entangled Clarence is a good preparation for his next exploit, which is directly presented on the stage in a scene coming between Clarence's imprisonment and death. The murder of Henry VI soon after the Battle of Tewksbury is described in the last scene but one of 3 *Henry VI*. The opening scene of *Richard III* refers to the long piping time of peace that has intervened since then, and Richard, bored by inactivity, seems to be eager for an exciting adventure. This opportunity is soon provided by Warwick's daughter, who in defiance of all reasonable calculations of time, comes out now to bury Henry VI's freshly bleeding corpse! Shakespeare takes yet another – though less outrageous – liberty with history. After the death of Henry VI and his son, Anne was for some time hidden away by Clarence and not married to Richard until the Warwick estates were divided, and Clarence was attainted and put to death five or six years after this marriage. Yet for no reason connected with his narrative, Shakespeare makes Richard woo Anne in a scene that comes between Clarence's imprisonment (I. i) and his death (I. iii).

What, one may ask, is the effect of these changes which,

obviously, were a part of Shakespeare's dramatic design? He minimizes all the other forces in order to bring out the extraordinary powers of his protagonist, making of the other figures – great and small – only stooges and puppets whom he directs and controls at his own sweet will. In the move against Clarence he is aided by Edward IV's declining vitality and the known opposition between the Queen's kindred and the King's brothers. And simple, plain Clarence proves clay in his hands. This is a good preparation for the next scene in which he plays against heavy odds. He was one of the assailants of Prince Edward, he is the butcher who, without assistance or incitement, killed Henry VI, and he now proposes to Anne, widow of one of his victims and daughter-in-law of the other! Time is a great healer, and one might say that Anne could gradually recover from her shock and marry the erstwhile enemy. But in Shakespeare's play the murder of Prince Edward is not three months old, and Henry's corpse is still bleeding when Anne, the chief mourner, confronts Richard. He takes all these liberties with history only to show how difficult a job Richard undertakes and accomplishes. For the historical Richard marriage with Warwick's daughter was an advantageous alliance that put him in part possession of the Nevil estates. Shakespeare's villain-hero discloses no such ulterior aim – he has a secret close intent never revealed – nor is he apparently fitted by Nature to court an amorous looking-glass. The wooing of Anne at a time when she is still in mourning for her first husband and father-in-law and full of curses for the murderer, is for Richard a game of skill which he undertakes and accomplishes with the virtuosity of a master. But although we may marvel at his cunning and his histrionic ability, we have been prepared for it by his success in the Clarence affair, which, aesthetically, if not chronologically, belongs to an earlier phase of his career.

While basing his account of Richard's rise to power on the accounts of Hall and Holinshed, which are derived from More, Shakespeare makes a significant change to which attention has been drawn by Herford and Dover Wilson. In the chronicles, the citizens of London are presented as intelligent and cynically incredulous, though they are powerless to thwart the mighty Protector. That is why Richard and Buckingham have to proceed with caution, and have first to make sure of the support of ambitious and unscrupulous men, 'diverse such as they thought mete to be trusted and likely to be enduced to that parte and hable to stand theim in steade, eyther by powre or by polycye'.[1] In *Richard III*, the commons are more docile than in history, and the Duke of Gloucester plays his nefarious game more easily because he has no real obstacle to get over. Dover Wilson thinks that Shakespeare makes this change because he was not interested in the constitutional question of the power and influence of the commons, and a more recalcitrant commons would have dis-ordered the play as he conceived (or constructed?) it. Further, 'Shakespeare was, at any rate in intention, a country gentleman, and nothing he writes elsewhere about the rising citizen class, or citizens in general, displays much sympathy for or understanding of them'.[2] In this tetralogy, Shakespeare shows an understanding of all classes and no sympathy for any one of them. Here kings and barons and their wives, bishops and commons are all agents and victims in a universal carnage. In this play the common people are not as unintelligent and uncritical as they are some-times thought to be. The Scrivener, who wrote out the indictment against Lord Hastings, knows very well that it is a faked document and wonders

> Who is so gross
> That cannot see this palpable device?
>
> (III. vi. 10–11)

In the next scene, Buckingham complains that the men whom he harangued on Richard's claims to the throne were unresponsive to his appeal and looked on 'like dumb statuas or breathing stones'. But such is the witchcraft exercised by Richard in the first three acts of the drama that everybody is ensnared, and the commons have no more power to resist him than had either Edward IV or Warwick's daughter Anne. Of the Citizens who gather to com-ment on state affairs after King Edward IV's death, one goes so far as to say that all the danger is to come from the Queen's kindred and expresses concern for the safety of the Duke of Gloucester; we need not, therefore, be surprised at the docility of the Mayor or the priests who supported Richard in his ascent to the throne, for they are no more or no less pliable than the Archbishops of Canterbury and York. It is only later on after Richard has reached his goal that his mind misgives him, his self-

---

[1] ibid., p. 364.
[2] Introduction to *Richard III* (New Cambridge Shakespeare), p. xxiii. Herford is referred to by Dover Wilson.

confidence is shaken, and the enormity of his crimes starts a chain of reactions that overwhelms him.

The mental ebullience Richard displays has been looked upon as a legacy from the Vice of the morality plays, an opinion which derives support from his own comment that he is like the formal Vice Iniquity. But although his mirthfulness, his dissimulation, his quibbling, his absolute lack of conscience – in the earlier stages – may remind one of the medieval Vice, there is a fundamental difference that testifies to Shakespeare's originality. As Charles Lamb noted long ago, Richard's 'unlaboured mirth' is different from the coarse, taunting humour, and clumsy merriment of a low-minded assassin, or we may add, of the medieval Vice, whose activities are controlled by the structure of the morality play.[1] Richard possesses a buoyancy or elasticity which is an end in itself and creates new and ever new situations for the sheer delight of self-expression. He wins Anne without telling us what particular advantages will accrue from the marriage, and he appears before a select body of Citizens with two bishops on either side for the sheer delight of a histrionic display, which, in view of the docility of the mob, was unnecessary. For a time he retains the same independence and unconcern even when things have begun to fall apart. Shakespeare's version of the Buckingham story is incomplete, because it does not adequately explain Buckingham's defection from Richard. Buckingham wanted the Earldom of Hereford, which Richard, contrary to an earlier promise, refused to grant; and Buckingham did not agree to the murder of the young sons of Edward IV, whom he, more than any one else, had helped to suppress. In history the alienation of Buckingham is satisfactorily motivated, for this Duke was allied to the Lancastrian house, and Hall notes that 'the tytle which he claymed by inheritance, was somewhat interlaced, with the tytle of Lancaster'. No wonder, therefore, that Richard 'rejected the dukes request with many spiteful, and minotary wordes'.[2] Shakespeare totally ignores the connexion between the Earldom of Hereford and the Lancastrian title. For his villain-hero it is enough that Buckingham has become 'high-reaching', 'deep-revolving' and 'circumspect', and having so long held out with him untired, has now stopped for breath. Once Richard has decided that he will not grant Buckingham's prayer, he proceeds in a characteristic

---

[1] *Richard III* (New Variorum, Philadelphia, 1909), p. 594.
[2] Hall's *Chronicle*, p. 382.

manner. It does not matter why he wants to marry Anne or why he refuses to redeem his promise to Buckingham. The wooing of the one and the baulking of the other are both expressions of his extraordinary mental resilience: he is in the conquering vein on one day and he is not in the giving vein on the other. That is the significant thing and to it all practical considerations are linked.

Many critics – most notably R. G. Moulton[1] – look upon *Richard III* as an elaborately wrought pattern of Nemesis. King Edward IV broke the oath he made when, after coming back from Burgundy, he said that he wanted nothing but his Yorkist possessions, and many thought that the murder of his young sons in the Tower was the result of this perfidy. In *Richard III*, Clarence, Hastings, and Buckingham – all are victims of the infernal, avenging Nemesis, of whom Margaret is the oracle. More than once they refer to the curse pronounced by Margaret, who has been introduced in this play, unhistorically, only because she is the best person to show how on the Yorkist side retribution follows sin. Dramatically, the most important thing is that Richard is a master player who uses the people around him as pawns on a chess-board, and he begins to falter as a player only when he loses his own alacrity of spirit. Many of his victims were themselves guilty of heinous crimes, and Margaret, who has the prescience of an oracle, can correctly foresee their catastrophic ends in the hands of a man whose character is partly or wholly hidden from their eyes. But this is only a by-product. What is of primary importance is the manner of his seduction of Anne, the deadly swiftness with which, under a veneer of lightheartedness, he proceeds to dispose of Hastings, the variety of artifices he adopts to win his way to the throne, the insouciance which does not altogether desert him even at the most critical moment. Although *Richard III* is an early work, we have the first glimpses of Shakespeare's maturer craftsmanship in the portraiture of Richard's extraordinary vitality, and the inexhaustible inventiveness that finds a fantastic connexion between Bishop Morton's strawberries and Hastings's death, and a far-fetched analogy between Buckingham's tedious prayer and the dull ticking of a clock. It is this quality that explains the great popularity of the play in Shakespeare's day, as also with succeeding generations of readers and play-goers.

Richard's one aim was to attain the throne, which he clearly articulates as soon as Edward, after convincingly defeating the

[1] R. G. Moulton, *Shakespeare as a Dramatic Artist* (Oxford, 1929), pp. 107–24.

Lancastrians, assumes the title of a king and expresses his desire to marry Lady Grey (3 *Henry VI*, III. ii). He dreamt on sovereignty even earlier when, before the Battle of Wakefield, he urged his father to break his oath and seize the throne:

> And, father, do but think
> How sweet a thing it is to wear a crown,
> Within whose circuit is Elysium
> And all that poets feign of bliss and joy.
>
> (I. ii. 28–31)

During his period of waiting and in all his manoeuvrings he never betrays that he has a conscience. Not that he is unacquainted with religion but he uses it only for his nefarious ends or for pure mockery. But there is a change soon after he attains his objective. That there is another side to his character is first hinted by his wife who, in giving an account of her miserable life, says:

> For never yet one hour in his bed
> Did I enjoy the golden dew of sleep,
> But with his timorous dreams was still awak'd.
>
> (*Richard III*, IV. i. 82–84)

These 'timorous dreams', however effectively Richard might have repressed them, must have influenced his waking life too, but the dramatist has not revealed the interaction between these two selves in the earlier stages of Richard's career. It is only when he is in the midst of his plans to get rid of his nephews that he suddenly awakes to a sense of sin:

> Murder her brothers, and then marry her!
> Uncertain way of gain! But I am in
> So far in blood, that sin will pluck on sin:
> Tear-falling pity dwells not in this eye.
>
> (IV. ii. 62–65)

But when in the past sin plucked on sin, he proceeded with complete unconcern as a man who had no awareness of the moral consequences of his actions. Here, on the eve of the murder of the Princes, Shakespeare accepts, for the first time, the scheme of the morality play in which sin is followed by remorse and retribution. Soon Richard rather hates himself and his conscience has a thousand several tongues of which every tongue brings in a several tale and every tale condemns him for a villain. This mental disturbance finds appropriate dramatic expression in the loss of his old zestfulness, in the necessity for sustaining himself with bowls of wine, and in the confused directions he gives in battle. In the earlier portion of the play, when Hastings and Buckingham had scruples of conscience and failed to give him the expected support, he had no sympathy for them, and did not even try to understand them. When Buckingham asked him what they were to do if Hastings remained faithful to Edward IV's young son, his reply was quick and sharp: 'Chop off his head' (III. i. 193). Buckingham's delicacy about murdering the imprisoned Princes is to him only an evidence of 'deep-revolving' circumspection, which shows that he scorns conscience without understanding it. When such a man suddenly holds himself guilty of murder, perjury and other several sins, the change does not seem to be either probable or necessary. The various 'shadows' that disturb him in his dream form a procession, but they are not dramatic in the true sense of the term, for there is no inner connexion between the man who mocked conscience and the man who is now mocked by it.

Although *Richard III* is an immature play, many of its scenes and situations are powerfully conceived, and it is Shakespeare's first attempt to organize the multifarious materials of history by placing the centre of interest in a tragic character. But the materials remain partly recalcitrant till the end. Although Richard is brought on the stage much earlier than history would permit, for a long time he is only the most powerful member of a compact group, without that 'aloneness' he afterwards asserts. Later, although Shakespeare passes over the Jane Shore episode made so much of in *The True Tragedie* and skips over the reign of Edward IV, the different episodes seem to stand out by themselves, and we look in vain for that spiritual cohesion and development that we find in Shakespeare's more powerfully conceived villains, in Iago and Macbeth. Indeed, *Richard III* raises the question, as does *Richard II*, whether a play can at the same time be a chronicle of events and a tragedy of character.

CHAPTER FOUR

King John

I

King John, written after the first tetralogy and possibly before *Richard II*, the first play of the second, cannot be counted as one of Shakespeare's mature works. Nor is it a popular play like *Richard III*, which belongs to the period of Shakespeare's apprenticeship. But when seen in the context of his development as a writer of historical plays, it is important because it not only marks an advance in characterization but also points the way to a new type of historical drama, in which the dramatist projects an idea through the interaction of plot and character. The morality plays of the Middle Ages personify abstract ideas and so does John Bale's *Kynge Johan*, the first historical play in English. Even if there is lively characterization here and there in these plays, it is the moral idea which comes first. In Shakespeare the primary thing is character, but in many of his plays, character and plot are linked to an emergent idea which develops along with them. It is not possible to have a drama without an idea but in some plays the idea is in the foreground whereas in others it runs like a subterranean stream beneath the structure of plot and character. We have faint beginnings of ideological drama even in 1 *Henry VI* and *Richard III*, but the first prominent specimen of it is to be found in *King John*.

It is generally thought that *King John* was based not directly on chronicle history, but on a play in two parts – *The Troublesome Raigne of King John of England* – which took its material from Holinshed and was partly influenced by John Bale's morality, *Kynge Johan*. The authorship of *The Troublesome Raigne* and its relation to Shakespeare's play are open questions. Some critics hold that *King John* was the earlier play and *The Troublesome Raigne* was derived from it, whereas some others look upon it as an earlier version of *King John*, made by Shakespeare himself. Yet another view points to an intermediate play between *The Trouble-some Raigne* and *King John*, but there is lack of agreement here, too, because one view is that this lost play, based on *The Troublesome Raigne*, was Shakespeare's source whereas others think that *The Troublesome Raigne* is largely a reported version of an early King John Play by Shakespeare. These questions, however, are not very relevant to the present context, because the dramatic significance of Shakespeare's *King John*, in its present form, will be revealed by a comparison with this anonymous play whether it is a source or an analogue or an early draft.

King John had various troubles after he came to the throne on the death of his brother Richard Coeur-de-Lion in 1199. First, his title was disputed by Prince Arthur, son of Geoffrey, his elder brother, although John had Richard's will on his side, and as the elder male representative of the royal line he was chosen King by the barons of England with the Archbishop of Canterbury and the Justiciar at their head. Such choice was not without precedent in those days, but Arthur, who was Duke of Brittany, was supported by the King of France and 'all the Nobles and men of Armes in Poictou'. In the quarrels and fights that followed, Arthur was taken prisoner, and as a prisoner he died in mysterious circumstances, a victim possibly of his uncle's murderous malice. When the Prince was kept a prisoner first at Falais, then at Rouen, Breton noblemen banded themselves together to have him set at liberty, and when they failed in their efforts at persuasion they 'began to levie sharpe wars against John in divers places'. When rumours about Arthur's death spread abroad, there was great commotion among the Bretons who started 'to make all the mischiefe they could devise'. After the conclusion of an inglorious treaty with France, as a result of which John surrendered all his French possessions north of the Loire, there began a long tussle between him and the Pope, in which John first asserted his independence and then tamely submitted to the authority he had set at naught. John also annoyed the English barons who had helped him to the throne; they now invited King Philip to invade England and forced John to grant the charter of rights, known in history as the Magna Carta.

The Troublesome Raigne and *King John* take sweeping liberties both in details and in the general outline of the story of this controversial king. The principal deviation is that in these plays events which were far apart are connected and even telescoped.

The episode of Arthur of Brittany ended with the death (or murder) of the Prince in 1203; the dispute with the Pope started only after Archbishop Hubert's death in 1205 and Cardinal Pandulph was not sent as a Papal legate until 1211. In 1214 the northern barons rose against John for his tyranny over them and this could have nothing to do with Prince Arthur whose cause was championed by the noblemen of Brittany and not of England. From the dramatic point of view, the chief contribution made by the author of *The Troublesome Raigne* was to mix up the affair of Arthur with the quarrel with the Pope and the revolt of the barons, who make the treatment of Arthur a part of their long complaint against John. Shakespeare, following the pattern set by the source play, shows his originality by simplifying the tangled materials; he is not interested in religious polemics or the baronial revolt but in portraying a character who stands for a new idea. *The Troublesome Raigne* gives a vivid picture of John's tyranny and criminality, but also presents him as a martyr and a tragic hero:

> *A Warlike Christian and your countreyman.*
> *For Christs true faith indured he many a storme;*
> *And set himselfe against the Man of* Rome,
> *Untill base treason (by a damned wight)*
> *Did all his former triumphs put to flight,*
> (Prologue)

But Shakespeare does not show a divided mind. He is not interested in religious propaganda. For him John is a bad king, but John's personal deficiencies only help him to develop his idea that the kingdom is more important than the king. The author of *The Troublesome Raigne* seems to be uncertain about John's title to the throne. He refers to Richard's will, to the 'consent' of the barons, and the Chief Citizen of Angiers, who may be said to represent neutral opinion, openly discounts Arthur's claim on the ground that he 'is but yong, and yet unmeete to raigne'. But John is also called a usurper by his enemies and Cardinal Pandulph incites Lewis to invade England, because he knows that John will get rid of Arthur and after Arthur he has a rightful claim:

> *Arthur* is safe, let *John* alone with him,
> Thy title next is fairst to *England's* Crowne:
> (*TR*, I. x. 1172–3)

John himself, when challenged by King Philip of France, cannot advance any argument except that of mere possession:

> Know King of *Fraunce*, I will not be commaunded
> By any power or Prince in Christendome,
> To yeeld an instance how I hold my owne,
> More than to answere, that mine owne is mine.
>
> (ibid. I. ii. 603–06)

In Shakespeare, there is no such ambiguity. Here King John is plainly a usurper, depending on strong possession rather than on rightful title. His mother speaks of a will only to be pooh-poohed by Constance. Nobody refers to his election by the barons or to Arthur's nonage. Rather Shakespeare puts Arthur's claims in a stronger light by representing Richard I as 'great forerunner of (Arthur's) blood'; the Prince himself is described as Coeur-de-Lion's 'posterity' and as Queen Elinor's 'eldest son's son', an error possibly deliberately made. Shakespeare wants to emphasize that Arthur was the rightful claimant backed by a foreigner who, after his death, invades England on his own account; whereas John is a criminal and a pretender, but in every sense an English king of England.

The same desire for simplification is noticeable in Shakespeare's other deviations from *The Troublesome Raigne*, which may be assumed to be his source. John crowned himself thrice in history, and in both the plays there is a scene of a second coronation which seems to be unnecessary to the assembled barons. In *The Troublesome Raigne*, the second coronation is intended to mark John's throwing off of the Papal yoke, but there are undertones in John's speeches that insinuate an additional motive:

> I grieve to thinke how Kings in ages past
> (Simply devoted to the Sea of *Rome*)
> Have run into a thousand acts of shame.
> But now for confirmation of our State,
> Sith we have proynd the more than needfull braunch
> That did oppresse the true wel-growing stock,
> It resteth we throughout our Territories
> Be reproclaimed and invested King.
>
> (*TR*, I. xiii. 1477–84)

It is in this scene that the Five Moons appear and Prophet Peter interprets the phenomenon as showing England's scorning 'the Sea and State of Rome'. But John's reference to the more than

needful branch here and to 'ambicious weedes' and 'false in-
truders' later on are a veiled suggestion that he has got rid of the
pretender to his throne, and when Hubert gives him the (false)
news of Arthur's death, he exclaims with a feeling of relief, 'Then
with him dye my Cares'. In Shakespeare's account, the second
coronation occurs after the consignment of Arthur to Hubert's
care; there is no reference to the domination of the Pope, and
the five moons are a mere symptom of the ominous atmosphere
produced by the rumour about Arthur's death. Dover Wilson
comments that Shakespeare takes considerable liberties with the
story of the coronation as told in *The Troublesome Raigne*, 'but
never makes clear why a coronation is required'.[1] It is, however,
the earlier version which is confused and ambiguous; Shakespeare
omits all references to the other motive in order to suggest that
previously John was crowned as a *de facto* sovereign, but now he
claims the throne by hereditary right. His own words are cryptic,
but suggestive:

> Some reasons of this double coronation
> I have possess'd you with and think them strong;
> And more, more strong, – when lesser is my fear, –
> I shall indue you with:
>
> (*King John*, IV. ii. 40–43)

His fear will become lesser when he has known that Hubert has
carried out his instruction and then the purpose of the second
coronation will become crystal clear.

The same thing may be said of the grievances of the barons,
which led to the granting of the Magna Carta. Shakespeare's play
can make no room for this charter of rights, because the lords as
presented by him have no complaints of their own and are moved
only by the death of Arthur, which they think was a murder
ordered by John. As Shakespeare views John's reign, the affair
of Arthur is of cardinal importance. It was for him that Philip
threw down a challenge to John and it is to avenge his death that
the lords welcome Lewis when he invades England. In *The
Troublesome Raigne*, the Bastard puts up a strong plea on behalf of
John, saying,

> For *Arthurs* death, King *John* was innocent,
> He desperat was the deathsman to himselfe,

---

[1] *King John* (New Cambridge Shakespeare, 1936), p. 158.

Which you to make a colour to your crime injustly
                     do impute to his default,
                                    (*TR*, II. iii. 456–8)

But in Shakespeare, he does not condone the crime; he suspects
Hubert grievously and knows that

> From forth this morsel of dead royalty,
> The life, the right and truth of all this realm
> Is fled to heaven, and England now is left
> To tug and scramble and to part by the teeth
> The unow'd interest of proud swelling state.
>   (*King John* IV. iii. 143–7)

Although he never overtly accuses John, he is too intelligent not
to realize who is really responsible for the crime. In *The Troublesome Raigne*, there is a mixture of two motives – the religious and
the secular. The troubles of England are due to the interference
of the Pope and to John's submission, forced as it is, to 'the Sea
and State of Rome'. John is no doubt largely responsible for the
tragedy of Arthur, but whatever his crimes may be, subjects, says
the Bastard, have no right to raise the standard of revolt against
the sacred majesty of a King:

> I say tis shame, and worthy all reproofe,
> To wrest such pettie wrongs in tearmes of right,
> Agaynst a King annoynted by the Lord.
>   (*TR*, II. iii. 461–3)

The two issues – ecclesiastical and political – lie apart, and the
principal defect of this play is that it lacks dramatic concentration
and unity of spirit. There is much greater cohesion in *King John*,
for Shakespeare reduces the importance of the religious issue to
the minimum and does not attribute any sacredness to the
authority of the King as one anointed by God. In his version the
Papal legate is only an instrument of aggression; he incites the
French King against John and later on urges the invasion of England
on Lewis to whom the Lords extend assistance in what one of them
calls 'the worship of revenge'. In all this Arthur remains the centre
of interest, because Pandulph starts the hostilities in which
Arthur is taken prisoner and Lewis can menace England only
because of Arthur's death. It is to be noted further that Shakespeare does not emphasize the scene of the Bastard's spoliation of
Church property and his King John dies without any prophecy of
the English Reformation on his lips.

While accepting the substance of his drama from *The Trouble-some Raigne*, Shakespeare makes many modifications which give a new significance to the story. Some critics, such as Richard Simpson and Lily B. Campbell, think that whatever the aesthetic value, the modifications were made with an eye to the political problems of Shakespeare's own time. The leading idea of Shakespeare's play, according to Simpson, is wholly connected with the crown; the problem is whether John deserves to be supported as King: 'The historical quarrel against John as a tyrant is changed into a mythical quarrel against him as a usurper aggravated by his murder of the right heir'. On this view Shakespeare took liberties with his sources – historical or dramatic – most probably to throw light on the problem of title to the crown, 'the standing trouble of Elizabeth's reign'.[1] Lily B. Campbell, who approaches the historical plays in the same spirit, finds here a close mirroring of the politics of Elizabeth's reign. The Arden Editor of *King John* listed the changes made by Shakespeare, noting 'above all, the close weaving together of the Papal interference, the death of Arthur, the baronial revolt as if brought about by Arthur's supposed murder, and the French invasion . . .';[2] and Campbell thus paraphrases the above summary: 'above all, the close weaving together of the Papal interference, the imprisonment and death of Mary, the revolt of the nobles as if brought about by Mary's imprisonment and death, and the Spanish attempt at invasion'.[3]

In Tillyard's opinion the specific problems dealt with in this play are the succession, which does not count for much, and the interrelated questions of the ethics of rebellion and the kingly character. Richmond was a rebel against Richard III, and since Richard III was a tyrant Shakespeare in that play seemed to justify rebellion. But John, though bad, argues Tillyard, is not a tyrant as was Richard, and the Bastard, in deciding to support him against the rebels, makes the right decision. 'It was better to acquiesce in John's rule, bad though it was, hoping that God would turn the King's heart to good and knowing that the sin of sedition would merely cause God to intensify the punishment, already merited, the country was in process of enduring'.[4]

Tillyard gives the Bastard an argument which the Bastard himself never puts forward. The Bastard never mentions God and

---

[1] *The Politics of Shakespeare's Historical Plays*, p. 402.
[2] Introduction to *King John* (Arden Shakespeare, London, 1925), p. xxvii.
[3] *Shakespeare's 'Histories'*, p. 136.
[4] *Shakespeare's History Plays*, pp. 225–6.

his punishments; he never says that John is bad or that John, though bad, is not a tyrant. He very eloquently condemns the crime of the murder of Arthur, does not try to exculpate John as does his prototype in *The Troublesome Raigne*, but he stops short there, and proceeds without a qualm of conscience to the thousand businesses that are brief in hand.[1] He tells the King of the defection of the lords, but not a word of the cause of the defection or of John's political or moral responsibility. When, later on, in a scene for which there is no parallel in the source play, Hubert brings the sad news of the precarious condition of the King who has been reconciled to the revolting lords, the Bastard exclaims, echoing Saint Paul:

> Withhold thine indignation, mighty heaven,
> And tempt us not to bear above our power!
>
> (*King John*, V. vi. 37–38)

Whom does he refer to as being tempted to bear above one's power? The King or the rebel lords? Possibly neither in particular, but it is significant that he does not pass any judgement either in defence or in condemnation. If John sinned, he was only tempted to bear above his power. The Bastard has not here a word of reproach even for Hubert. Obviously his mind is projecting itself to the many businesses that are pressing upon him. Beyond John, this realist, who is inspired by an ideal, visualizes something that is greater than royalty. His interest in John as a person is not altogether eclipsed for he wants to remain John's servant still, but except for the cryptic lines quoted above, he does not say a word about whether John deserved his misfortune or whether there was any substance in the complaint of the rebels who sinned against their mother country. Neither does he seem to be particularly worried about the succession; he assigns to the new King only the duty of waiting upon his father's funeral. It is immaterial whether the dramatist had Arthur or Mary, the French or the Spanish invasion in mind; the fact remains that he does not express anywhere any firm opinion on the moral or political issues of John's reign or Elizabeth's. Indeed, his treatment of political and ethical problems is as half-hearted as his presentation of the religious conflict that raged in England in John's reign as in the Tudor age.

---

[1] We may contrast him with Hector who says:

> 'Tis mad idolatry,
> To make the service greater than the god;
> (*Troilus and Cressida*, II. ii. 56–57)

Other critics, also with a didactic turn of mind, make light of John and base their interpretation of the play on the portrait of the semi-historical Bastard who dominates the events dramatized. But they too give an over-idealized view of their hero's character, ignoring its contradictions and superficialities. Middleton Murry, in what is possibly the most brilliant essay on the subject, finds in the Bastard's taunting of Austria – 'And hang a calf-skin on these recreant limbs' – the quickness of his natural sympathy, and then proceeds to exculpate him of the charge of conniving at the killing of Prince Arthur by saying that he cannot believe that the King would command a murder so devilish.[1] For this belief, however, the text offers no justification. Equally unwarranted is Middleton Murry's inference that the Bastard distinguishes the voice of innocence in Hubert.[2] He at first defends the man against Salisbury's intended attack, but soon overcome with emotion he loads him with curses, for he suspects him very grievously. When Hubert finishes his plea of innocence, there is nothing to show that he believes even a fraction of it and he curtly asks him to bear away the dead body. Even now he has no illusion about John's title to the throne:

> Now powers from home and discontents at home
> Meet in one line; and vast confusion waits, –
> As doth a raven on a sick-fallen beast, –
> The imminent decay of wrested pomp.
>
> (IV. iii. 151–4)

There is no doubt in his mind that John has 'wrested' the pomp that rightfully belongs to Arthur, but he is also intent on upholding it. In real life, as in great drama which reflects and explores it, men act from mixed motives, and cannot, in the heat of action, stop to pursue a line of thought to its logical extreme. When he meets the King after Arthur's death, the Bastard's attitude to the affair remains significantly undecided:

K. John – Would not my lords return to me again
           After they heard young Arthur was alive?
Bast. –   They found him dead and cast into the streets,
           An empty casket, where the jewel of life
           By some damn'd hand was robb'd and ta'en away,

---

[1]*Shakespeare* (London, 1954), p. 166.
[2]ibid., p. 168.

K. John – That villain Hubert told me he did live.
Bast. –   So, on my soul, he did, for aught he knew.

(V. i. 37–43)

He nowhere repeats the plea put forward by the Bastard in *The Troublesome Raigne* that Arthur 'desperat was the deathsman to himselfe'. Whatever the value of Hubert's protestation of innocence, the Bastard does not budge from his conviction that some damned hand – and who but the King employed it? – robbed Arthur of life. He knows what everyone knows and passes beyond the shameful act to the great thoughts that stir him more than the King; he has no time either for moral casuistry or for criminal investigation.

II

At every step the Bastard derives a lesson from his observation of the world, and his cynical but tolerant attitude colours his observation and helps him to evolve a code of conduct which, although rooted in Commodity or Self-interest, is yet passionately idealistic. Convention makes him lay claim to Sir Robert Faulconbridge's lands, but he knows that he is really an illegitimate son of King Richard I. When he finds that even the King's mother has the same suspicion, he does not dream, as does the Bastard in *The Troublesome Raigne*, but accepts the logic of facts in a spirit of reckless adventure. Like Hall's Dunois on whom he is modelled, he has 'a mounting spirit', but also a contempt for climbing, smooth-faced courtiers amongst whom his new-made honour places him. A realist, he forgives his mother because he knows – the comparison is fantastic – how difficult it is for a mere woman to hold her own against the impetuous advances of a King whose fury the aweless lion could not resist. But although unashamed of his bastardy, he does not defend it with the salacious arguments advanced by Edmund in *King Lear*. When he comes to France, he is a soldier of fortune but also a keen-eyed realist who sees through pretences of all kinds. The Duke of Austria is a coward who flaunts a trophy he did not win by valour; he is like the hostess of an inn, who, ignorant of fighting herself, hangs out the sign of Saint George and the Dragon. Equally contemptible are the Citizens of Angiers, who without realizing the risks involved in warfare 'Talk as familiarly of roaring lions as maids of thirteen do of puppy-dogs'. Their defiance of the mighty claimants to their allegiance is as unreal as his own calling his brother's father 'dad'. Nor has he any respect for the Kings ranged on either side, who, forgetting their professed aims, are easily persuaded by him to a temporary truce so that they may raze the city by means of their united assault. This would seem wild counsel to men guided by firm principles but not in the mad world of John, Philip, and Lewis. Lewis is a vile lout – Shakespeare makes nothing of the suggestion that the Bastard is in love with Blanch – drawn and hanged and quartered in the amorous looks of a girl, and King John and King Philip easily modify their attitudes for the sake of Commodity or Self-interest.

The Bastard has awareness of moral values, but he finds that in a crooked world principles are seldom adhered to. He reviles Commodity, but knows that he will woo it as soon as he gets the opportunity. Gradually he chalks out an ideology of his own, which might be described as broad-based expediency, in which self-interest is merged in the interest of the nation. In the wordy duel between the Pope's legate and King John, he remains more or less silent, for he cannot follow Pandulph, who in the name of religion, wants to grab temporal power and is supported by the cowardly Duke of Austria and the unprincipled King of France. Neither can he put in a word for John, who, himself a usurper, opposes the Pope's 'usurp'd authority' and talks glibly of 'the free breath of a sacred king'. But when France falls from England, his common sense as well as self-interest tells him that John's cause is his and 'France shall rue for it'.

Although gifted with penetrating intelligence, he is more a man of action than of thought and delights in nothing so much as in riding a storm. After finishing the first bout of fighting, he returns to England 'to shake the bags of hoarding abbots'. Arthur's death – he is too intelligent not to see that it is murder – gives him a rude shock and for a moment he stands amazed. But when 'heaven itself doth frown upon the land', there is no time for mourning or recrimination, and he hurries forth to take up the work that lies ready to his hand. He knew very well that Arthur was the rightful heir to the English throne but could not support him so long as the prospective English king was only an instrument in the hands of the rulers of France and Austria; now he cannot join the other lords to avenge the young Prince's death, for it has been followed by foreign aggression on English soil. That is the secret of his unswerving loyalty to John. Tillyard thinks that the Bastard is 'the true upholder of the great principle of Degree',[1] but this does not take note of the basic difference between the problem facing him and the situation that occasions Ulysses's great speech on the subject in *Troilus and Cressida*. There is no question of opposing rights between Agamemnon, the leader of the Greeks, and Achilles, their most powerful general, and the Greeks are them-selves aggressors on foreign soil. If the Bastard had really been interested in Degree, he would, consistently with his convictions, have asked John to surrender the 'pomp' he had 'wrested' from Arthur.

Like many other men of action, the Bastard does not start with a fully formed philosophy; rather whatever philosophy he has he discovers in the heat and bustle of action. It would be wrong to say that he has to decide between the sin of sedition and the dis-honour of serving a bad master. The problem does not present itself to him in that way at all. The great speech he delivers in front of Arthur's dead body does not contain any personal reference to John. The images he uses – dogged war bristling his angry crest for the bare-picked bone of majesty and vast confusion waiting like a raven on a sick-fallen beast – only show the deep disgust the contest for succession has aroused in him. But beyond the rival claimants and their tugging and scrambling, lies the land that is greater than problems of title and 'degree'. The foreign invasion helps him to carve out his philosophy of life. It was implicit in the support he accorded to John in spite of his con-viction that Arthur symbolized 'The life, the right and truth of all this realm', but he becomes fully conscious of it only under the stress of a national crisis. When inspiring John to assert himself, he says:

> Be great in act, as you have been in thought;
>
> (V. i. 45)

But John has not been touched by great thought in any crisis. He does hurl defiance at the Pope (III. i.), but the Bastard, though present then, does not say a word; possibly he knows John and can dimly visualize the later surrender, or he is un-interested in the theological controversy about supremacy between the King and the Pope. The greatness of thought – as of action – is his rather than the King's; John has receded into the background and is now no more than a symbol or an instrument of the Bastard's

---

[1]*Shakespeare's History Plays*, p. 220.

idealism. When the King complacently speaks of a compromise which he hopes will be effected by Pandulph, he breaks forth into a passionate outburst:

> O inglorious league!
> Shall we, upon the footing of our land,
> Send fair-play orders and make compromise,
> Insinuation, parley and base truce
> To arms invasive? shall a beardless boy,
> A cocker'd silken wanton, brave our fields,
> And flesh his spirit in a war-like soil,
> Mocking the air with colours idly spread,
> And find no check?
>
> (V. i. 65–73)

It is 'our land' with 'our fields' and 'war-like soil' that has replaced in his imagination the King who for the moment sways the sceptre there. The lords who have joined the foreign aggressor he appropriately describes as

> bloody Neroes, ripping up the womb
> Of your dear mother England,
>
> (V. ii. 152–3)

It is in this larger loyalty that his personal loyalty to John is merged. He would be less than human if he did not revenge John's foul murder, but his main business is now

> To push destruction and perpetual shame
> Out of the weak door of our fainting land.
>
> (V. vii. 77–78)

When the new King thanks the lords in a flood of tears, he cuts short such sentimental exuberance by saying that they should pay the time no more than 'needful woe' and then proceed to the larger task lying ahead. The philosophy of life he has now arrived at is a creed of unselfish patriotism; but, although far from the doctrine of Commodity he enunciated earlier, it has its roots there. At Angiers he saw before him everyone feathering his own nest and compromising or sacrificing principles. He is more or less detached but he makes the right choice in defending John against his enemies, for John's cause is the nation's. What he sees instinctively at the beginning of the play he later on elaborates into a philosophy, which is justified by the experience of the revolting barons, and in this way the different strands of the story are welded into a unity.

III

King John, it has already been pointed out, is an interesting experiment in a new type of historical drama, being at the same time a history play and a drama of ideas. It puts at the centre of the action a character only dimly historical, and it diverges so violently from its ultimate chronicle source that critics call it an unhistorical medley and not a history play at all. But if we look upon it as a drama of ideas, the liberties taken with history need not be seriously disturbing. The main incidents – Arthur disputing John's title, the French King's championship of Arthur's cause, the liquidation of Arthur, the defiance of and surrender to the Pope, the French invasion, and John's inglorious death – are all true to history or tradition. Not so plausible is the basic idea of English nationalism, which is more Elizabethan than medieval. But, appropriately enough, the exponent of this new creed is a man who is only incidentally mentioned in the chronicles but who leaps into life in Shakespeare's play for the simple reason that here Shakespeare is unburdened by recorded facts. The Bastard makes explicit what was implicit in medieval life. Shakespeare partly anticipates the method, later adopted by Bernard Shaw, of endowing a character drawn from the Middle Ages with a keen awareness of what people of those days must have felt half-consciously, for that is the only way, argues Shaw, in which the past can be intelligibly interpreted to the present. The things the Bastard is represented as saying are exactly the things the historical Bastard would have said if he had been conscious of the implications of his own actions.

Another criticism which has already been touched on is that it is difficult to reconcile the Bastard's worship of Gain and Commodity with his appreciation of the nobler values of life, his realization of the tragedy of Arthur with his indifference to it. But we must remember that he is essentially a man of action whose vision is never obscured by introspection. He is not deeply interested in any question so long as it is confined to the field of theory. But as soon as there is a pressing necessity for action, he rises to the occasion with vigour and intrepidity and in the course of action works out an adequate philosophy. A more justifiable criticism of both the conception and construction of the play is the growing unimportance of John, the titular hero, who is unimpressive in the first half of the play and becomes more or less a passenger in the later stages where he is so much overshadowed by the Bastard that Shakespeare does not even adequately explain the Monk's motive in poisoning him. That is why, as Reese points out, the play seems to lack a focal point, for the man whose interests are at stake plays second fiddle to the man who protects those interests.[1] Although this criticism is largely true, the defect complained of is a part of Shakespeare's basic conception of the play as the evolution of an idea. The historians and other writers whom Shakespeare consulted or might have consulted were sharply divided in their opinions; for Catholics John was Nature's enemy, a monster who would put hell to shame, whereas for Protestants in the Tudor era he was a harbinger of the Reformation and a martyr. Shakespeare, who is primarily a dramatist and no propagandist, does not pander to any prejudice, Catholic or Protestant. Nor would the Great Charter appeal to him as a dramatic subject here, even if he were aware of its political significance, for his theme is not popular (or baronial) liberty against royal tyranny, but the evolution of patriotism out of concrete, living experience, and for this the man who protects John's interests without being directly involved in them is obviously a better hero than John who fights only to defend his own 'usurp'd authority'. Thus the principal limitation of this play as a personal tragedy is a part of its strength as a drama of ideas.

[1] *The Cease of Majesty*, p. 261.

CHAPTER FIVE

The Second Tetralogy

H. I 1599

I

CRITICS are divided over the question whether the two tetralogies form a single unit or not. Some think that they not only
portray history continuously from the last years of Richard II to
the death of Richard III at Bosworth Field but also give a connected
view of the events which are their theme. Others hold that the
two sets of plays were written at different times and are thema-
tically different. There is internal evidence that Shakespeare,
when writing his second tetralogy, was mindful of his work in
the first, but it is also true that there is little similarity between
the incidents represented in the two tetralogies. According to the
second of the two schools mentioned above, the problems dealt
with in the first group of plays are all the off-shoot of civil dissension, whereas in the second group the main question is one of
succession, what type of ruler should occupy the throne of England – after Elizabeth. The interpretation of both the schools is
irrelevant to the dramatic significance, which is independent of
the purely political implications of the story, and it is doubtful
if such political implications are deducible from Shakespeare's
dramatization of history. The first tetralogy presents three kings –
Henry VI, Edward IV, and Richard III. Of these, Henry VI is
portrayed as virtuous but weak, Richard III as powerful and vil-
lainous, and both as unfit to rule. But Edward IV was an able ruler,
and Hall describes his reign as prosperous. Why, then, if Shakespeare were really interested in the problem of kingship, does he
pass swiftly over the piping time of peace that was ushered in by
Edward IV? In the second tetralogy, Richard II is whimsical,
tyrannous, and weak, but Shakespeare's presentation of his character is not totally unsympathetic. Nor can any clear lesson be
gleaned from his portraiture of Henry IV who is crafty but competent. Henry V is, indeed, a king among men and a man amongst

kings. But he succeeded partly because his father smoothed the
way for him by quelling one rebellion after another and handing
over the crown as a hereditary possession descending legitimately
from the father to the son. This is made clear in Henry IV's dying
address to the Prince who is unduly eager to ascend the throne:

> God knows, my son,
> By what by-paths and indirect crook'd ways
> I met this crown; and I myself know well
> How troublesome it sat upon my head:
> To thee it shall descend with better quiet,
> Better opinion, better confirmation;
> For all the soil of the achievement goes
> With me into the earth. It seem'd in me
> But as an honour snatch'd with boisterous hand,
> And I had many living to upbraid
> My gain of it by their assistances;
> Which daily grew to quarrel and to bloodshed,
> Wounding supposed peace. All these bold fears
> Thou seest with peril I have answer'd;
>
> (2 *Henry IV*, IV. v. 182–95)

We cannot, therefore, separate the glorious days of Henry V
from the unquiet time of Henry IV, nor can we dissociate them
from the dissensions with which the country was torn after him,
for the simple reason that these dissensions were a sequel to his
victories. As Prince, Henry V could not have been unacquainted
with the plea put forward on behalf of Mortimer, but on ascending
the throne he failed to gauge the motive that really incited the
Earl of Cambridge. This blindness was partly responsible – though
Shakespeare does not explicitly state the connexion – for the
disasters which fell upon England after his death. The French
victories of Henry V were a glorious episode in English history,
but they were no more than an episode.

> Small time, but in that small most greatly liv'd
> This star of England,

says the Chorus in the Epilogue, where we are also reminded that
the effect of the victories was short-lived, for the many lords
who managed the state after Henry V's death lost France and made
England bleed. The fact that this same Chorus compares Henry V's
return from France with Essex's return from Ireland suggests that
Shakespeare was not thinking of the type of ruler that should

occupy the throne but simply of a splendid military adventure made by a competent general.

Nor will it be correct to say that he wants in this tetralogy to dramatize Hall's view of history and connect the disasters of England with Henry IV's usurpation which sowed the seeds of dissension, though that view is expressed here and there, sometimes in casual hints, and sometimes eloquently, as by the Bishop of Carlisle in *Richard II*. In the speech in which the dying Henry IV exhorts his son 'to busy giddy minds/With foreign quarrels', he admits that he won the crown by by-paths and indirect crooked ways and prays for God's forgiveness. But the son who is about to ascend the throne has no such scruples and accepts his inheritance as a matter of right:

> My gracious liege,
> You won it, wore it, kept it, gave it me;
> Then plain and right must my possession be:
> Which I with more than with a common pain
> 'Gainst all the world will rightfully maintain.
>
> (2 *Henry IV*, IV. v. 219–23)

He will be disturbed by qualms of conscience at a later date, when, at Agincourt, he will face the supreme crisis of his life. He would be more than human if he were not so troubled when his fate hung in the balance. On other occasions his conscience is not so sensitive, and his intelligence is introspective only by halves. A detailed examination of Henry V's character will be taken up in the proper place. Here it is necessary to point out that although critics have found many similarities between the political problems in the reign of Elizabeth and the problems that occurred in the stretch of history from Richard II to Richard III, they have not noticed certain basic dissimilarities. Henry V was an English king who reigned for about ten years, but it is not so much how he governed England as how he successfully initiated a military adventure in France that is the subject-matter of the concluding play of the series. Since the tetralogy ends with a warning about the disastrous consequences that followed his brief success, it could as well be read as a morality on the wrong type of kingship, which begins with a riotous youth and ends with foreign conquest that succeeds for a short period but is followed by disastrous after-effects. There is no limit to which moralistic interpretation of Shakespearian drama cannot be carried.

II

It is on account of this didactic bias that contradictory inter-
pretations have been made – ever since the time of Shakespeare –
of *Richard II*, which has been looked upon as both a plea for and a
warning against rebellion. That Richard II was guilty of serious
misgovernment is undoubted, but did he deserve to lose his
crown? And even if he so deserved, had Bolingbroke the right to
depose him, or had his subjects any right to try him? Various
answers are given to these questions by various dramatic characters, and the most reasonable view is to take these answers as
characteristic of the speakers – as, indeed, they almost always are
– rather than as expositions of a particular view of history or
politics. The principal commentators on men and events, besides
the Bishop of Carlisle, whose opinions have already been referred
to, are the King's uncles – Lancaster and York – and the philosophical Gardener. When we meet Gaunt in this play, he is no
longer the formidable warrior of whom Falstaff speaks in 1 *Henry
IV*; he is old and dying, more a prophet inspired than a man of
action. That is why although he condemns the murder of his
brother the Duke of Gloucester, and later says that if Edward III
had had any foreknowledge of Richard II's misdeeds he would have
deposed the latter before he had been possessed, Gaunt does not
himself want to lift a finger to revenge his brother:

> God's is the quarrel; for God's substitute,
> His deputy anointed in his sight,
> Hath caus'd his death; the which if wrongfully,
> Let heaven revenge, for I may never lift
> An angry arm against his minister.
>   (*Richard II*, I. ii. 37–41)

This is characteristic of a dying old man who speaks bitterly but
cannot act, and his comments need not be taken as Shakespeare's
interpretation of history. Even in the Mowbray-Bolingbroke
affair, he is too old to take any effective part, and here it is out of
pity for him, and not with an eye to the public, as reported by
Froissart,[1] that King Richard reduces Bolingbroke's banishment
from ten years to six. The prophetic but ineffective Gaunt is a

---

[1] *The Antient Chronicles of Sir John Froissart*, p. 514.

dramatic contrast to his vigorous son who does not philosophize, but acts.

The King's other uncle, the Duke of York, is 'neuter' and may represent Shakespeare's views as much as Gaunt – and better. York first stands for the principle of order or 'degree', which critics look upon as the basic theme of Shakespeare's historical plays. After Gaunt's death, he stands for Hereford's rights, because Hereford may come to possess his father's properties by the accepted law of succession:

> Take Hereford's rights away, and take from Time
> His charters and his customary rights;
> Let not to-morrow then ensue to-day;
> Be not thyself; for how art thou a king
> But by fair sequence and succession?
>
> (II. i. 196–200)

When Bolingbroke, taking the law into his own hands, repeals himself and comes back to England, York acts very comically indeed. He at first uses violent language against Bolingbroke – he has no other weapons – and then in spite of being Richard's deputy, professes neutrality. Later, when Bolingbroke, violently disrupting 'degree', ascends the throne, he becomes a loyal subject of the usurper and even regards the usurpation as a part of divine dispensation:

> But heaven hath a hand in these events,
> To whose high will we bound our calm contents.
> To Bolingbroke are we sworn subjects now,
> Whose state and honour I for aye allow.
>
> (V. ii. 37–40)

Now he finds 'some strong purpose' of God in the cold and hostile reception the people gave to King Richard! Since Shakespeare makes such a spineless, vacillating old man an exponent of the philosophy of order, his own attitude to that philosophy cannot be without an element of irony.[1]

If there is any scene in the play which may be regarded as symbolically suggestive, it is the one (III. iv) in which the Gardener and his servant moralize on their commonwealth. The Gardener is equally hard on

---

[1]Another exponent of order or 'degree' is the contemptible Rosencrantz in *Hamlet* (III. iii).

> too fast growing sprays,
> That look too lofty in our commonwealth,
>
> (ll. 34–35)

and on

> The noisome weeds that without profit suck
> The soil's fertility from wholesome flowers.
>
> (ll. 38–39)

The noisome weeds are Wiltshire, Bushy, and Green, but is not Bolingbroke a too fast growing spray that disturbs the peace of the commonwealth? The best way to interpret this scene would be to ignore its political overtones and emphasize only its dramatic significance. The comments made by Gaunt and York are characteristic of old men who are supposed to have authority but are powerless to act. The Gardener is a representative of the common men who had cooled towards Richard and whose attitude is graphically described later on by the Duke of York:

> As in a theatre, the eyes of men,
> After a well-grac'd actor leaves the stage,
> Are idly bent on him that enters next,
> Thinking his prattle to be tedious;
> Even so, or with much more contempt, men's eyes
> Did scowl on Richard: no man cried, 'God save him';
>
> (V. ii. 23–28)

The Gardener is too refined and contemplative to be classed with those barbarians whose 'rude misgovern'd hands' threw dust and rubbish on King Richard's head, but he expresses their point of view, speaking 'no more than every one doth know'. Richard allowed noisome weeds to suck the soil's fertility from wholesome flowers, and no wonder if

> He that hath suffer'd this disorder'd spring
> Hath now himself met with the fall of leaf;
>
> (III. iv. 48–49)

Not that the Gardener is an exponent of the philosophy of rebellion any more than of order; he only accepts the change from 'plume-pluck'd Richard' to mighty Bolingbroke as inevitable.

Richard II is best read as a human drama rather than as a political document or as a moral homily. It is a personal tragedy like Richard III, that is to say, the emphasis is more on the declining fortunes of a single protagonist than on the course of events, or the social picture, or the development of any idea. Although the play deals with the reign of Richard II, there is no mention of the Peasants' Revolt or of Wyclif and the Lollards. There are critics who think that the tragic denouement in this play is 'explicable only through the action of Fortune's sightless wheel, in whose motion consisted the medieval idea of tragedy'.[1] But by making Richard personally responsible for his disasters, Shakespeare seems to stress his independence of the medieval idea of tragedy and show in the true Renaissance spirit that man is the architect of his fate and not a victim of the blind goddess Fortune. Even in the opening scene, Bolingbroke, in defying Mowbray really accuses Richard of shedding the blood of a near kinsman:

> Which blood, like sacrificing Abel's cries
> Even from the tongueless caverns of the earth,
> To me for justice and rough chastisement;
> And, by the glorious worth of my descent,
> This arm shall do it, or this life be spent.
>
> (I. i. 104–08)

Abel was murdered by his brother Cain, and everyone could see who played Cain's part here. Mowbray's defence is vague but it further incriminates Richard:

> For Gloucester's death,
> I slew him not; but to mine own disgrace
> Neglected my sworn duty in that case,
>
> (ibid. 132–4)

thus showing that whoever murdered Gloucester, the directive came from the King. In this scene, it is not merely his criminality that is brought to light but also his weakness, his powerlessness to command the militant lords to silence. When we meet him next at the lists at Coventry, a medieval tournament is described in all its elaborate detail. But what is dramatically significant is that it is utterly unnecessary, for Richard and his Councillors decide that the combat must not take place.[2] The scene shows

---

[1] M. M. Reese, *The Cease of Majesty*, p. 227.

[2] In Froissart the King's Councillors see him a few days prior to the day of combat and force him to stop the trial and impose life-long banishment on Mowbray, and a ten years' exile on Bolingbroke, to be reduced later on to six years. Shakespeare follows Hall and Holinshed in making the King throw down his warder when the combat is about to begin and then consult his Council for two hours – represented, in the play, by the Folio stage direction of 'A Long Flourish' – and he accepts with modification Froissart's account of the reduction of Bolingbroke's sentence; in Holinshed the sentence is reduced only at a later stage (Vol. II. p. 848). Is the prevention of the combat a sudden whim or a pre-meditated move? Whatever view we may make of this, the episode is an unnecessary theatricality exposing a weakness of Richard's character.

that he enjoys a dramatic situation as an end in itself and must have relished his own somewhat piquant role – he can banish but not 'atone' the contestants – in it.

Richard has observed the tremendous farewell given by the common people to Bolingbroke, and himself says, rather prophetically, that it seemed that the whole of England were in reversion Bolingbroke's. But, strangely enough, he allows himself to be persuaded that he need not worry about Bolingbroke and proceeds to confiscate Gaunt's property. He is both a bully and a coward. When there are powerful people before him, he cowers and cannot face a critical situation, but he is churlishly arrogant to a dying uncle and has no scruple about seizing what belongs to a man whom he has himself exiled and whose popularity he has observed.

When he returns from Ireland, there is a sea-change in his attitude to life, of which the only hint he had earlier was his love for theatrical shows. The rash young man who acted arrogantly and sometimes treacherously, has now become a poetical dawdler. Shakespeare follows history faithfully, reproducing the different stages of Richard's downfall – the conspiracy at home and abroad, the disloyalty of the peers who weighed the scales in favour of Bolingbroke, the desertion of the Welsh troops, the hostility of the common people, the march to London, the trial and the deposition. But he completely transforms the chronicle narrative by placing at the centre of the action – or inaction – a dreamer who gives away a kingdom in order to be able to luxuriate in his griefs. In vain does Carlisle, the best of his supporters, urge him to rally his forces and meet the enemy. He now sees himself in a new light and is content to contemplate his own downfall. He was a believer in the divine right of kings, which no subject could touch. If that magic will not work, he is no more than a man and has no right to call himself a king:

> throw away respect,
> Tradition, form, and ceremonious duty,
> For you have mistook me all this while:
> I live with bread like you, feel want,
> Taste grief, need friends: subjected thus,
> How can you say to me I am a king?

> (III. ii. 172–7)

How this poetical fantast lay concealed behind the arrogant wastrel of the first two acts has not been represented in course of the action.

That is the only thing 'enigmatic' about Richard's character, and the greatest defect of the drama *as* drama. But it is this trait in his character, a pure invention of Shakespeare, which explains his catastrophic end. Lamb speaks of the reluctant pangs of abdicating Royalty,[1] but are the pangs entirely 'reluctant'? Rather it seems that his griefs are a commodity which pleases as much as it galls him. When he says to the usurping Bolingbroke:

> I thank thee, king,
> For thy great bounty, that not only giv'st
> Me cause to wail, but teachest me the way
> How to lament the cause,
>
> (IV. i. 299–302)

he is not entirely ironical.

In Holinshed, Northumberland is sent by Bolingbroke to the King at Conway, and the King is brought to Flint Castle, virtually a prisoner. After this he is held fast in the mighty hold of Bolingbroke; and the reception accorded by the people, as the two potentates journey to London, makes it clear that the deposition, which comes off without delay, will be a mere formality. Indeed, the feeling against Richard is so strong that if he were not committed to the Tower, worse things might happen:

'Manie evill disposed persons, assembling themselves together in great numbers, intended to have met with him, and to have taken him from such as had the conveieng of him, that they might have slaine him. But the mayor and aldermen gathered to them the worshipfull commoners and grave citizens, by whose policie, and not without much adoo, the other were revoked from their evill purpose.'[2]

By means of slight changes here and there, Shakespeare transforms the above episode and makes Richard primarily responsible for his deposition. Although he has received some rude shocks – the departure of the Welsh army, the beheading of his favourites by Bolingbroke who has repealed himself – his cause is not irretrievably lost, and both Carlisle (III. ii) and Aumerle in Flint Castle (III. iii) think that he may yet consolidate his forces. But even before Richard comes to Flint Castle, he describes himself as the slave of woe, and when he meets Bolingbroke at the base court of the Castle,

---

[1] *Specimens of English Dramatic Poets*, &c. (London, 1885), I, p. 31.
[2] *Chronicles*, II, p. 859.

> Sorrow and grief of heart
> Makes him speak fondly, like a frantic man:
>
> (III. iii. 184–5)

No wonder that although Bolingbroke at this stage claims only his Lancastrian possessions and Richard has no idea of what the London mob will do, he speaks of deposing himself and refers to his cousin as King Bolingbroke.[1] In Holinshed's narrative, although the King is more or less a prisoner, at Flint Castle he promises no more than that the Duke will enjoy all that is his, without exception.[2] But Shakespeare's Richard makes a characteristic addition:

> Your own is yours, and I am yours, and all.
>
> (ibid. 197)

Yet another interesting modification is that whereas in the chronicle narratives charges are first preferred and considered in Parliament and then the King is persuaded to resign, in Shakespeare's play Bolingbroke is busy investigating in Westminster Hall the murder of his uncle the Duke of Gloucester when he is interrupted by the following announcement made by the Duke of York:

> Great Duke of Lancaster, I come to thee
> From plume-pluck'd Richard; who with willing soul
> Adopts thee heir, and his high sceptre yields
> To the possession of thy royal hand.
>
> (IV. i. 107–10)

And Bolingbroke answers:

> In God's name, I'll ascend the regal throne.
>
> (ibid. 113)

It is only after this that Richard is fetched to Parliament House

> that in common view
> He may surrender;
>
> (ibid. 155–6)

and the importance of the reception by Londoners is so much

---

[1] In Holinshed, Northumberland musters his army before the King's presence at Conway and then ambushes and arrests him (pp. 856–7). In Froissart's account, Flint Castle is surrounded by a vast body of Londoners before Bolingbroke meets Richard. Significantly enough, Shakespeare leaves out these items from his version.

[2] p. 858.

minimized that it is only later reported by the Duke of York to his Duchess.

The question has very often been debated whether Boling-broke's seizure of the throne was the climax of a carefully planned campaign, or whether he only accepted a 'reversion' he did not originally aim at. In the sources – in Holinshed as well as in Frois-sart – Bolingbroke was promised assistance by the nobility as well as the prelacy 'if he expelling King Richard, as a man not meet for the office he bare, would take upon him the scepter, rule and diademe of his native land and religion'.[1] The poet Samuel Daniel, too, says that he at first proceeded warily seeming not to affect that which he did effect.[2] Shakespeare omits all such suggestions, and in view of the fact that he has based his play on Holinshed and Froissart and might have been acquainted with Daniel's poem, the omission seems to be deliberate. 'Was Shakespeare', says R. F. Hill, 'trying to show Bolingbroke, as Dover Wilson puts it, as "borne upward by a power beyond his volition", or was the suppression designed to achieve the ambiguity of a politic usurper? All the clues point to the second alternative'.[3] But there may be a third alternative which does not exclude the first two and shows them to be not indeed incompatible. Bolingbroke – whatever his supporters in the chronicles might have thought – does return in the play only to claim his patrimony, but he is a normally am-bitious man and behaves as such a man might be expected to behave. He thinks of the murder of Richard only after the Oxford conspiracy makes him realize how dangerous a living deposed king might be for his successor. Such a thought would not, of course, come to a really pious man, but Bolingbroke is too worldly-minded to be really pious. It is also characteristic of him that after the murder of Richard, he asks for God's pardon for this woeful act, but he does not think that there was anything illegal or immoral about his assumption of royalty. He has, how-ever, a very unquiet time as king, and finds that even if the deposi-tion of Richard was justified, he has little to say to those who make out a case for Edmund Mortimer, Earl of March. *Henry VI* has more than one reference to the Mortimer claim, and one of the reasons why the Percies raise the standard of rebellion in

---

[1] ibid., p. 852: the commonalty also joined the agitation, and, according to Froissart, the Archbishop of Canterbury was sent to Bolingbroke 'from the inhabitants of London and other councils of England'.
[2] Daniel: *Civil Wars*, Book I, st. 94.
[3] *Early Shakespeare*, p. 107.

Henry IV is that the Earl of March – Shakespeare, following Holinshed, makes a confusion between the uncle and the nephew – has a better title to the throne than Bolingbroke. It is significant that there is not the faintest reference to this subject in *Richard II*, where even the Bishop of Carlisle, Bolingbroke's most unsparing critic, does not advance any plea on behalf of the line of the Duke of Clarence. It is evident that in *Richard II*, Bolingbroke has no scruples of conscience about gaining the crown, for his ambition and the occasion fit into each other, and considerations to be urged afterwards are not mentioned at all. When later he speaks of the by-paths and indirect, crooked ways by means of which he wormed his way to the throne, he has the same kind of hindsight that Hamlet displays when he exclaims before the Ghost:

> O my prophetic soul!
> My uncle!
>
> *(Hamlet*, I. v. 40–41)

Or it is like the illumination that comes, more dramatically, to Emilia, when after the exposure of Iago's conspiracy, she is at first puzzled and then exclaims:

> Villany! villany! villany!
> I think upon't, I think, I smell't; O villany!
> I thought so then, I'll kill myself for grief.
>
> *(Othello*, V. ii. 188–90)

Departing from Hall's view of Henry IV as the first author of the civil strife that later on raged in England, Shakespeare presents him in this play as a man who seizes the crown but is no usurper because his ambition grows with his opportunities and the crown is to him more a gift than a prize won by force or diplomacy.

III

Historical plays deal not with one action but with periods of time covering a multiplicity of incidents. Such periods may – as in *Henry V* – be given an effective unity through the reigning monarch who is supposed to be connected with all that happens during his time. Still drama is not history and requires greater concentration than is found in a chronicle of events. That is why the playwright focuses attention on one important action, presented as the central theme of a long reign. Such is the deposition of Richard in *Richard II* or the emergence of English nationalism under the impact of foreign invasion in *King John*. When the dramatist cannot bring within a single view all the events which happened during the time of a particular monarch or his successors, who belonged to the same epoch, he distributes his materials over separate plays that are linked to each other as items in an extended series. Such are the three parts of *Henry VI*, which tell a story that is rounded off in *Richard III*. The plays in this tetralogy or trilogy – if *Richard III* is left out – are bound to one another by the survival of some characters from one play to its successor or successors and by an all-embracing, if somewhat loose, unity of sentiment. In spite of this unity, every play is a separate entity with its own central theme which may be considered without reference to what has gone before or will come after. The dramatic interest is enriched if one play in the trilogy of *Henry VI* is related to its companions, but one never thinks that the three parts constitute a single play in fifteen acts. No part is felt to be incomplete without a reference to its successor and each part is intelligible without the help of its predecessor.

But can the same thing be said of the two parts of *Henry IV*? Ever since the eighteenth century critics have been divided in their opinions about the relationship between the First Part and the Second. Some have taken the two plays as a single unit of ten acts divided into two halves only for the convenience of stage representation. Others think that the First Part is complete in itself, and that Shakespeare had originally no intention of writing the Second Part when he planned the First. It was the success of the first story of Prince Hal and Falstaff which made him continue it in another play. The main argument for supposing that the two plays are structurally a unified whole is that the story of Prince Hal and Falstaff ends inconclusively in 1 *Henry IV*, where the Prince redeems himself but does not reject his loose companions. The Prince's ultimate intention is clearly indicated in the second scene of this play, 'which', as Dover Wilson puts it, 'looks forward not only to the coronation of Henry V but also to the rejection of Falstaff, neither of which occurs until the very end of Part 2'.[1] An additional argument is the rebellion of Northumberland and Archbishop Scroop, which is just mentioned in the First Part and elaborated in the Second. The principal argument on the other side is that 'structurally 2 *Henry IV* is almost a carbon

---

[1]Introduction to 1 *Henry IV* (New Cambridge Shakespeare), p. x.

copy of the first play'.[1] Besides this structural similarity, the Second Part repeats many of the motives and incidents of the First, which it would not have done if the two plays had been conceived as a unity. There is estrangement between the King and the Prince in the First Part, and they are reconciled at the end of the play. But in the Second Part 'the clock is turned back most flagrantly'; 'we find them estranged all over again so that they must be reconciled a second time'.[2] Then, again, the meeting of Westmoreland with the Archbishop and other rebels is partly a repetition of the earlier embassy of Sir Richard Blunt, and Falstaff's recruiting adventure in the Second Part is only an elaboration of the damnable misuse of the King's press, which he speaks of in the First. Would Shakespeare have thus repeated motives and situations and represented a second redemption of the Prince if he had thought of the plot as a unity?

In what is perhaps the most illuminating contribution to the subject, Harold Jenkins suggests the third alternative that Shakespeare possibly first thought of writing a single five act drama, depicting the defeat of Hotspur, the rejection of Falstaff and the accession of Henry V, but when this play was half way through, that is to say, when it had reached the Third Act, his plan expanded, and 'a new pattern can be seen emerging during the fourth act'.[3] The earlier story of Henry V, as conceived by Shakespeare, has two important episodes which merge into one. Henry asserts his real self by defeating Hotspur and rejecting Falstaff. In the two part play as we have it now the adventures of Falstaff take twice as much time as the episode of Hotspur, which is finished in the First Part. But that is not the impression we gain in the first three acts of 1 Henry IV, where 'the Hotspur-plot and the Falstaff-plot show every sign of moving towards their crisis together'. But from about the beginning of the Fourth Act, Falstaff and his men are pushed into the background, and the Battle of Shrewsbury is 'built up into a grand finale in its own right'.[4] The Falstaff story is given prominence again in Part II, but this also partly destroys its dramatic effect. After the Battle of Shrewsbury Prince Hal cannot any longer present 'a headstrong front'; but he comes unreclaimed into Part II, and thus the two parts, although complementary, are also incompatible.

---

[1]M. A. Shaaber in *J. Q. Adams Memorial Studies*, p. 221.
[2]ibid., p. 222.
[3]*The Structural Unity of Henry IV* (London, 1956), p. 21.
[4]ibid., pp. 15, 221.

Whenever the Second Part might have been planned or written, *Henry IV* is, aesthetically, a unity, and its theme is not so much the education of Henry V – in fact, he requires no education at all – as the Fortunes of Falstaff. Whatever might have been Shakespeare's original intention, the central figure is neither the old King nor the lean Prince but the fat knight. Falstaff creates a bubble of a world, which, in spite of much that is morally reprehensible or physically loathsome, is a beautiful, many-coloured bubble, and the tragedy of this comic world is that it is not viable. Falstaff is a symbol of the unrepressed instincts of humanity, which thirst for fulfilment, rebel against repression and are anxious to preserve life rather than risk danger and death. Fighting is not unwelcome, because it is exciting and may bring unexpected – and undeserved – rewards. But Falstaff has no illusions about honour, which, being insensible, cannot see or hear and belongs only to the dead. D. A. Traversi traces the unique appeal of Falstaff to his traditional and popular derivations, to the many anonymous figures, consecrated by popular custom, which went into the making of this great figure of swelling, if unregulated, vitality and comic vigour.[1] But what he and other critics forget is that although odds and ends of traditional characters may be found in Falstaff, he is in every sense an original creation, and it is his originality more than his derivative traits that should engage our attention. He is grey Iniquity, a clown and a buffoon, but above everything else he is, both in theory and practice, an exponent of a philosophy of life, the philosophy which glorifies the primal instincts above reason and morality. From this point of view, even his age, about which there are no precise data, has a symbolic significance. He was born about three o'clock in the afternoon, but we do not know anything about the day or year of his birth. He represents the elementary instincts that are anterior to reason and morality and to old father antick the law with his rusty curb. But although he can defy age and make fun of disease, he misjudges the forces that restrain and yet nourish social life, and at the end pays dearly for his miscalculation.

From this point of view, *Henry IV* may be called a drama of ideas, but it is not a morality play in which man – here the young Prince – is tempted by Vice in the person of Falstaff and then rescued by Government and Law represented by the King and the Chief

---

[1]Derek Traversi, *From Richard II to Henry V* (London, 1961), p. 76. Other critics are cited by Harold Jenkins. (*Shakespeare Survey*, Vol. 6, p. 15).

Justice. It is wrong to speak of Falstaff as a misleader of the Prince, because the Prince is never misled. In the all-important soliloquy at the end of I. ii, which has already been discussed, he says that his mixing with the roisterers is no more than an occasional holiday; but it is not even that, for he mixes with these people only with the hidden intention of throwing them off and gaining credit for an amazing reformation, for

> nothing pleaseth but rare accidents.
> So, when this loose behaviour I throw off,
> And pay the debt I never promised,
> By how much better than my word I am
> By so much shall I falsify men's hopes;
> And like bright metal on a sullen ground,
> My reformation, glittering o'er my fault,
> Shall show more goodly and attract more eyes
> Than that which hath no foil to set it off.
> I'll so offend to make offence a skill;
> Redeeming time when men think least I will.
>   (I. ii. 229–39)

This shows that although he speaks of 'reformation' and of 'Redeeming time',[1] these phrases are not really applicable to him. Even if we 'take Hal's soliloquy as a conventional device intended to make the audience wiser in this matter than all other persons in the play', we have to notice the content of the 'wisdom' Shakespeare communicates to us in advance. Not only in this soliloquy but also in his conversation with Poins, to whom he opens his mind, Henry shows no affection for Falstaff. It is, therefore, difficult to agree with Dover Wilson when he says that 'the mainspring of the action is the choice . . . he is called upon to make between Vanity and Government, taking the latter in its accepted Tudor meaning, which includes Chivalry or prowess in the field, the theme of Part I, and Justice, which is the theme of Part II'.[2] In Shakespeare's play, the Prince never regards himself as faced by two alternatives, and he is not called upon to make a choice. In fact, he deceives both parties – his father as well as Falstaff. In Part II, Falstaff has an interesting conversation with the Lord Chief Justice, in which his lordship expresses the commonly accepted opinion about the relationship between the old knight and the young Prince:

---

[1] That this is not the theme of the two plays is also proved by Falstaff's constant parody of repentance and 'conversion'.

[2] *The Fortunes of Falstaff*, p. 17.

Ch. Just. – You have misled the youthful prince.
Fal. – The young prince hath misled me : I am the fellow with the
        great belly, and he my dog.

(I. ii. 165–8)

Falstaff's words have a deeper significance than he is himself aware
of. It is the Prince who misleads Falstaff and is like a dog taking a
fat, blind man to an abyss. And in a different way the Prince misleads other people also who think that his loafing about with
Falstaff is a part of his real self.

The two parts of *Henry IV* will appear to be a single unit structurally, if we put Sir John at the centre of the action. This may
seem to be repugnant to Shakespeare's original design, because
both 1 *Henry IV* and 2 *Henry IV* are historical plays, and Falstaff
has only a slender connexion with history, if he can be said to
have any connexion with it at all. But whatever Shakespeare's
intentions might be, there is no doubt that Falstaff is the most
engrossing character in the two plays, which in their successive
stages reveal different facets of his personality. As pointed out by
Shaaber, the principal difficulty in seeing the two plays as one is
that the clock is turned back most violently in the Second Part.
In 1 *Henry IV*, the Prince redeems himself on Percy's head, and it is
expected that he will not return to his loose companions. But in
the Second Part, he seems eager to 'commit/The oldest sins the
newest kind of ways', and is again estranged from his father, which
means that the Second Part is a repetition and not a continuation
of the First. The explanation offered by some critics that the
reconciliation effected in 1 *Henry IV* is of a 'tentative' nature is
unacceptable, because unsupported by the text. At Shrewsbury,
the Prince fully rises to the occasion and shows that his follies are
like a garment he can throw off at will. Though he is still good-
humouredly tolerant towards Falstaff, for whom he will 'gild' a
lie, if it does any grace to the fat knight, he acts so heroically and
is such complete master of the situation that his relapse into
tavern life in 2 *Henry IV* seems, indeed, to be incompatible with
what has gone before. But we do not feel the incompatibility,
because the subject of the two part drama is the revelation of
Falstaff and not the reclamation of Prince Hal, who was never
grafted to the barren society he was occasionally 'match'd withal'
as a recreation or as a screen to hide his real greatness. The
Prince can without effort leave Eastcheap tavern and 'Rise from

the ground like feather'd Mercury', and then with equal ease –
this may be another justification for the repetition in the Second
Part – he passes from Shrewsbury to his former companions and
gives the Lord Chief Justice a box on the ear. The Prince is only
a 'factor' for bringing out the infinite variety in the character of
the man whom he mixes with and then discards. The different
scenes in this ten-act-drama unfold the different elements which
are mixed in Falstaff and make of him not a man, but a phenomenon. He flies from Gadshill but not from Shrewsbury, where
he does not fight Hotspur but coolly shams dead and escapes
scoring upon the pate. His encounter with the Lord Chief Justice
is more frontal, because his adversary is a man of words and not of
the sword, and in skirmishes of wit no man – not even the Prince
– is a match for him. Here there is no repetition and no incompatibility.

The Prince would not reject Falstaff until he came to the
throne. Before that the fat rogue might be an occasional nuisance,
but he was never a serious impediment until, under Hal as King,
he could claim the laws of England as at his commandment. In the
First Part, Falstaff jocosely speculates about the merry time he
and his fellow-Corinthians will have when Hal becomes king, and
the Prince equally jocosely says that he will certainly banish him,
but until he ascends the throne it is all a joke. When at Shrewsbury Sir John lies down as if he were dead, the Prince exclaims:

> Poor Jack, farewell!
> I could have better spar'd a better man.
> O! I should have a heavy miss of thee
> If I were much in love with vanity.
> Death hath not struck so fat a deer to-day,
> Though many dearer, in this bloody fray.
> (1 *Henry IV*, V. iv. 103–08)

He is not in love with vanity; so he will not 'have a miss' of
Falstaff now or afterwards. But the time for rejecting him has not
yet arrived, for we are in the middle of the story – in history as well
as in drama. The Battle of Shrewsbury, with which the First
Part ends, occurred in history in the early years (1403) of Henry
IV's reign (1399–1413). But Shakespeare puts it designedly in the
middle, for he makes Henry IV's death follow immediately after
the suppression of the revolt of Archbishop Scroop (1405), which
is mixed up with the Battle of Bramham Moor (1408), where

Northumberland was defeated and killed. The framework of the plot shows that the end of the First Part marks the middle point in the story of Henry IV as Shakespeare dramatically envisaged it.

Such a framework is admirably suited to the revelation of Falstaff's intricate personality, which is the inner substance of the two plays. He is an old man when the play opens, but his age is not made prominent in the First Part. Rather his joining younger men in a robbing expedition and the alacrity with which he rushes to the battlefield only show his mental and physical vigour unbedimmed by age. But in the Second Part, as pointed out by Traversi, 'he is given an altogether new burden of lechery, age, and disease, a burden which undoubtedly justifies in part his treatment at the hands of Prince Hal'.[1] What is more important than moral justification is that the picture of Falstaff in the Second Part prepares us for the final Rejection, and although we may sympathize with him, we feel here, more insistently than in the First Part, the impact of a new world – represented by Prince John and the Chief Justice – in which he is a misfit. It is a world of serious people, and his tragedy is that although gifted with a subtle intellect he does not realize that even Prince Hal, who drinks sherris sack in his company, really belongs with these soberminded boys and men rather than with a pot-valiant knight like him.

Critics have noted a change – rather a deterioration – in Falstaff's character and position from the First Part to the Second. Middleton Murry, for example, thinks that in the Second Part he is carried on rather than re-created, that even in the most important scenes in which he appears in this play, his presence is rather felt than manifested.[2] I have elsewhere shown that this charge is without foundation, that except in the last scene Falstaff's intellect is as alert and resilient in the Second Part as in the First.[3] Dover Wilson notices a change of theme from Chivalry in the First Part to Government in the Second. This, too, is only partly true. There is, indeed, very little of chivalry in the Second Part, where Prince John puts down rebellion not by honourable fighting but by shameful chicanery, but it is not true to say that Law or Government does not appear in the First Part at all. There it is represented by the Sheriff who comes to investigate the

[1]*Scrutiny* (XV, No. 2, 1948, Cambridge), p. 125.
[2]*Discoveries* (Saint Giles Library, London, 1940), pp. 61–62.
[3]*Shakespearian Comedy* (O.U.P. Ind., 1961), pp. 261–2.

Gadshill robbery and to arrest Falstaff, just as in the Second Part it is represented by the majestic figure of the Lord Chief Justice. In both the plays Falstaff escapes the long arm of the law, and his own cleverness is more in evidence in Part II, where he twice faces the Chief Justice and outwits him, than in Part I, where, with an amazing control of nerves, he himself goes to sleep, leaving the Prince to dispose of the Sheriff. But there is a change in tone and atmosphere, which is relevant to a study of the structure of the plays. In the First Part, the Prince is a merry young man unburdened with cares of government. Falstaff can, therefore, create his own world of *joie de vivre*, where the Sheriff comes as an intruder and is curtly dismissed. Falstaff is unperturbed; even death by hanging would be an excellent sport which the spectators would enjoy. When the Prince calls him a natural coward without instinct, his answer is characteristic:

> I deny your major. If you will deny the Sheriff, so; if not, let him enter: if I become not a cart as well as another man, a plague on my bringing up![1]
>
> (1 *Henry IV*, II. iv. 551–5)

But in the Second Part the Chief Justice more than once makes a determined attack on him, rating him soundly for his misdeeds, and although in the early stages Falstaff parries the attack with inexhaustible mental agility, he does it only for the moment; we are reminded that it is the unquiet time, and not his capacity for bluffing and blustering, that has enabled him to overpost the Gadshill action. But that is about as far as he can go, and the Chief Justice warns him not to wake the sleeping wolf of law.

There are other suggestions that re-inforce the impression that in the new world in which Hal will become king, Falstaff will have no place. He always needs money; in the First Part he robs passers-by as merrily as he misuses the King's press, and the Prince pays his bills and stands surety when ready money is not available. But things are different in the Second Part, because the Prince has been separated from him, and Master Dombledon from whom he wants two and twenty yards of satin, demands better assurance than Bardolph's bond and his. Naturally Falstaff is worried about the eternal consumption of the purse for which he cannot find adequate remedy. He has another worry, for old age brings with

---

[1]In Part II, Death is a grim reality: '. . . do not speak like a death's head: do not bid me remember mine end'.

it the burden of disease, and his gout and his pox have begun to
play the rogue with his great toe. He tries to laugh it away but
cannot, for he has to consult a doctor about his water. In one
respect, he has amazingly, though also rather amusingly, staved
off the decay incidental to old age, for he is still lecherous like a
young rake. Nowhere does he show greater vitality than in his
meeting with Doll Tearsheet, a young fleshpot, who thinks him
to be as valorous as Hector, worth five Agamemnons, ten times
better than the Nine Worthies, and loves him better than she
loves ever a scurvy young man of them all. But the emphasis is as
much on the inexhaustible vitality of Falstaff as on the incongruity
of this conjunction of Venus and Saturn, for the bombard of sack
is now likened to a dried elm, a withered elder, who should
have long outgrown his amorous impulses. There is another point,
which, although somewhat trivial, is not without significance.
The Prince did not join the Gadshill robbery in the same spirit as
Falstaff but he did join it. He does not, however, know Doll
Tearsheet or of the connexion between her and Falstaff, which
shows how wide is the gulf that now separates the boon companions of Part I. The punishment given by the Beadle to Doll in
V. iv is a foretaste of the judgement pronounced on Falstaff in the
last scene of the play. It is through such hints as well as by the
widening rift between the Prince's world and Falstaff's that
Shakespeare prepares us for the final Rejection, which was first
broached in the second scene of the First Part. Falstaff tries his
best to evade the corrosive effect of age, disease, and covetousness,
but it become increasingly clear that he stands outside the moral
world of duty and responsibility which Prince Hal is soon to
enter.

The end is suggested in another way, which, if somewhat
devious, throws light on Shakespeare's craftsmanship. Although
Falstaff has little direct contact with King Henry IV, their worlds,
curiously enough, seem to move in unison. In the First Part,
Falstaff is in a triumphant mood and so is the King. The King has
worries, but they cannot ruffle him. He meets the rebels in the
Council Chamber and rebukes them; he offers them terms which
they refuse and then he defeats them convincingly in open battle.
Falstaff, too, outwits the Prince and Poins by his story of two men
in buckram turning into eleven, by keeping clear of the Sheriff
and then by his exploits in the Battle of Shrewsbury. In the Second
Part, the King is weighed down by his worries and suffers from

insomnia. Falstaff's spirit rises superior to the ills of the flesh, but he cannot get rid of his gout and his pox, and added to these he has financial troubles which seem to have no end. Here the King is too sick to take part in battle, and his younger son – Prince John of Lancaster – quells rebellion not by any feat of heroism but by sheer treachery which leaves a bad taste in the mouth. Falstaff's world, too, has lost its former brightness. His flirting with Doll Tearsheet is as loathsome as it is comical. Although his vivacity is unclouded, he is old, old, for the youthful exploits of the company to which he belonged were performed more than half a century ago, when Shallow was at Clement's Inn and he was page to Thomas Mowbray, Duke of Norfolk. It is, therefore, dramatically appropriate that the Rejection of Falstaff comes close on the heels of the death of the old King. The new King rises Phoenix-like out of the ashes of two worlds, one of them conscience-ridden, and the other untroubled by conscience.

Prince Henry, who assumes the title of Henry V, is the most dominating figure in the second tetralogy, but he has aroused the most opposed reactions amongst readers and critics. Romantic critics, who have been bewitched by Falstaff and outraged by the Rejection, have looked upon him as a vulgar worshipper of success. 'Whatever terror', says Hazlitt, 'the French in those days might have of Henry V, yet to the readers of poetry at present Falstaff is the better man of the two'.[1] Yeats and Masefield are more forthright in their condemnation of him.[2] For them he is a man who conforms to type, he is successful just because he has a commonplace mind. On the other hand, recent critics of Shakespeare, who look upon the two parts of *Henry IV* as a political morality, hold that in the Prince the dramatist tries to represent the type of man who deserves to be king, a sophisticated hero with a comprehensive mind, an Olympian detachment and an experience of all sorts of people and things. Such in outline is the view presented by Dover Wilson, Tillyard, Ribner, and others.[3] Prince Hal does not appear as a character in *Richard II*, but is referred to as an unthrifty young man who hangs over his father like a plague. When we meet him in the second scene of 1 *Henry IV*, he is a gad-about passing his time mostly with unrestrained

---

[1]*Characters of Shakespeare's Plays* (W.C. No. 205), p. 167.
[2]Yeats: *Ideas of Good and Evil* (London, 1914), pp. 107 ff. John Masefield: *Shakespeare* (H.U.L.), pp. 111–13, 121–2.
[3]Tillyard, however, detects a falling-off in his character in *Henry V*.

loose companions, but as we see more of him our first impressions are modified, until at the end of 2 *Henry IV* he emerges as the sun from the clouds and thus reproves the man who is supposed to have misled him:

> I know thee not, old man: fall to thy prayers;
> How ill white hairs become a fool and jester!
> I have long dream'd of such a kind of man,
> So surfeit-swell'd, so old, and so profane;
> But, being awak'd, I do despise my dream.
>
> (V. v. 52–56)

It is worth speculating whether Shakespeare wanted to present a political-ethical ideal in revealing the different aspects of the Prince's character. That he had some such purpose seems to be arguable, for there are certain things about Hal which have no immediate dramatic significance. In *Richard II*, Bolingbroke suddenly asks Percy (and other lords) where his 'young wanton and effeminate boy' might be. And when Percy gives a very uncharitable picture of the Prince's activities he stops the conversation equally abruptly and unaccountably, saying

> As dissolute as desperate; yet, through both,
> I see some sparkles of a better hope,
> Which elder days may happily bring forth.
>
> (V. iii. 20–22)

The initial reference to the Prince is uncalled for, and one wonders on what grounds Bolingbroke bases his concluding hope. In 2 *Henry IV*, the ageing, care-worn King is generally bitter towards his eldest son, but his first comments are very flattering:

> For he is gracious, if he be observ'd:
> He hath a tear for pity and a hand
> Open as day for melting charity;
> Yet, notwithstanding, being incens'd, he's flint;
> As humorous as winter, and as sudden
> As flaws congealed in the spring of day.
> His temper therefore must be well observ'd:
> Chide him for faults, and do it reverently,
> When you perceive his blood inclin'd to mirth;
> But, being moody, give him line and scope,
> Till that his passions, like a whale on ground,
> Confound themselves with working.
>
> (IV. iv. 30–41)

K

Here is a description of the Prince which is not reflected in the dramatic action. Where does he shed his tear for pity or reveal his hand open as day for melting charity? Indeed, in this very scene, a few lines ahead, the King is full of grief at the dissolute ways of his son, who, he thinks, will never be able to wean himself from low company. But the above description, addressed to an unimportant character, shows that Shakespeare intended to portray in Prince Hal not, indeed, a type of the man without blemish, but of the large-hearted hero in whose character there is room for faults and humours but whose greatness is not darkened by them.

Whatever intentions Shakespeare originally might have had, we have to see how far these have been woven into the fabric of the drama. In other words, it is not the portrait Shakespeare intended to draw but the portrait which emerges from the two plays that is of primary importance. We meet the Prince first in 1 *Henry IV* (I. ii), when he is with Falstaff and his crew; but although he is with them he is not of them. With little originality in himself, he seems to be here only an instrument for bringing out the exceptional quality of Falstaff's wit and imagination. He makes verbal onslaughts on Falstaff, but these only serve to throw into prominence the richness of Falstaff's mind. The Prince's best things are a weak imitation – or 'damnable iteration' – of the fat rogue's sallies, and as the play proceeds his inferiority becomes more and more manifest. In 2 *Henry IV*, Falstaff, who is critical of everybody, including himself, makes a shrewd comment on the Prince and Poins, who in spite of surface differences seem to him to be very much alike:

'. . . and such other gambol faculties a' has, that show a weak mind and an able body, for the which the prince admits him: for the prince himself is such another; the weight of a hair will turn the scales between their avoirdupois.'

(2 *Henry IV*, II. iv. 272–7)

By a 'weak mind', he means one that is inferior to his own. Not that the Prince is not intellectual, but his mind is not creative, not 'apprehensive, quick, forgetive', and what is equally significant, it does not possess the capacity for understanding others. The plan of outwitting Falstaff in the Gadshill expedition is devised by Poins and not by the Prince, who has such a limited insight into the character of Sir John, Bardolph, and Peto that he asks if these fellows will not be 'too hard' for them! Poins and the Prince think that at the end they will be able to refute Falstaff's lies and that will be the virtue of the jest, little realizing that his incomprehensible lies will put their truth to shame. The much-discussed soliloquy at the end of I. ii shows that the Prince cannot enter into the amoral world of Falstaff, and he is also incapable of self-criticism. He is self-complacent and self-centred and never examines the justness of his own way of life or how unfair he is to the man whose unyoked humour of idleness he upholds for a while. If Falstaff deceives himself by wishful thinking, the Prince engineers that deception by cold calculation. From the alacrity with which the Prince passes from the tavern to the battlefield, Falstaff should have, one might argue, realized the essential difference between their attitudes. But Falstaff, who had no knowledge of the soliloquy which gives us the proper orientation even at the beginning of the play, might be excused for thinking that the Prince's serious business of fighting and politics is only a diversion from their sports. The ironical undertones we detect in the Prince's comments and retorts escape Falstaff, not because he is fat-witted but because the Prince deliberately misleads him.

Sir John's superior inventiveness is shown as much by the amazing transformation of two men in buckram into eleven as by his successive impersonations of the King and the Prince in the mock interview staged by him in the tavern. The idea, once again, is not the Prince's but Falstaff's; it is he who transfigures a tavern chair into his canopied throne, a paltry cushion into his crown, and plain Mistress Quickly into his tristful queen. And the two speeches he delivers on behalf of himself are a marvel of creative advocacy. When he makes out an eloquent plea ending with an exhortation not to banish plump Jack, the Prince can only tamely retort, 'I do, I will', words which have a grave import in the light of the final Rejection, but have little force in the present context. The Prince's mental inferiority is shown in the speech in which, as King Henry, he dwells on Falstaff's unsuitability as a companion for himself, and speaks, indeed, like 'the most comparative, rascalliest sweet young prince' Falstaff described earlier. The commonplaceness of his mind is made still more prominent on those rare occasions when he tries to make himself merry in Falstaff's absence. The most glaring example is when he jests at the expense of the Drawers with their limited vocabulary. Here we come across another unpleasant trait of his character, which obtrudes itself on other occasions too – his consciousness of his own superiority in rank. Although he treats Poins as a friend, he never forgets the difference in status between them. His behaviour towards his father shows him as a princely hypocrite – the epithet is coined by Poins – an accusation which he says he wants to avoid. It is keeping vile company that has taken from him all ostentation of the sorrow he professes to feel. Later on, when his father is – too hastily – supposed by him to be dead, it is the crown that first attracts his attention. He addresses it as 'polish'd perturbation' and 'golden care', but when with unseemly eagerness he snatches it and leaves his father's death-bed, there is little sign of either perturbation or sorrow. His tears are formal tears which are his father's due, as the crown is his own rightful legacy from his father.

Although the Prince is deficient both in emotion and imagination, he has a strong will and a cold, calculating intellect, which combine to give him exceptional practical ability. Essentially unimaginative, he does not idealize honour in the manner of Hotspur, but he is the better soldier of the two and he knows it. He was never defiled by Falstaff's company and can banish him without a qualm of conscience. This is the picture that emerges from the two parts of *Henry IV* – not of a soul of courtesy or of love or honour, but of a competent but somewhat impassive man who knows his worth but is lacking in both self-criticism and sympathy. He will not leap or dive to gain honour, but neither will he win victories in the shameful manner adopted by his brother. He will not only use his own giant strength but also

> choose such limbs of noble counsel,
> That the great body of our state may go
> In equal rank with the best govern'd nation;
> That war or peace, or both at once, may be
> As things acquainted and familiar to us;
>
> (2 *Henry IV*, V. ii. 135–9)

Is the portrait a satire, whether deliberate or unintended, on practical ability that wins success, on heroism that is essentially unheroic? It may be going too far to say that there is an undertone of sarcasm or irony in a portrait that is professedly epical, but the suggestion made by such critics as Yeats, Masefield, and others is not altogether excluded. Adopting two phrases made famous by Granville-Barker, we may say that in *Henry IV* the 'daemonic'

Shakespeare has already begun to appear behind his more 'complaisant' self.[1]

IV

The epic spirit is emphasized more fully in the final play of this tetralogy, which portrays Henry V's French success 'as a great upward sweep in the history of England'. Here Shakespeare, through the Chorus, protests against the limitations of the stage, and makes out a plea for epic drama that ignores the conventions imposed by neo-classic criticism. In the Prologue to *Every Man in His Humour*, Ben Jonson severely criticizes the loose structure of *Henry VI* and the artificial unity achieved through the Chorus in *Henry V*:

> with three rustie swords,
> And helpe of some few foote-and-half-foote words,
> Fight over *Yorke*, and *Lancasters* long jarres:
> And in the tyring house bring wounds, to scarres.
> He rather prayes, you will be pleas'd to see
> One such, to day, as other playes should be.
> Where neither *Chorus* wafts you ore the seas;
> Nor creaking throne comes downe, the boyes to please;
> Nor nimble squibbe is seen to make afear'd
> The gentlewomen; nor roul'd bullet heard
> To say it thunders; nor tempestuous drumme
> Rumbles, to tell you when the storme doth come;
> But deedes, and language, such as men do use;
> And persons, such as *comoedie* would chuse,
> When she would shew an Image of the times,
> And sport with humane follies, not with crimes.

Although there might be other Elizabethan plays that would answer the above description, the reference to Shakespeare's histories is unmistakable. But Jonson quite misses the point in *Henry V*, which, in spite of its sporting with human follies and crimes, is not a comedy but an experiment in the fusion of epic and drama. That is why the Chorus here is not only exultant but also explanatory, even apologetic. The functions of the Chorus, as summarized by John Munro, are (i) to exalt the minds of the audience to an appreciation of the might and glory of Henry V, (ii) to apologize for the limitations of both stage and author, (iii) to

---

[1] *Aspects of Shakespeare* (British Academy Lectures), pp. 49–83.

lead the audience to interpret the stage figures as 'ciphers to this great accompt' and jump over time and space; (iv) to give the audience notice of events that take place off the stage, and (v) to look into the future effects that should and will arise from the events represented.[1]

The true purpose of the Chorus is not so much to give unity to the play as to indicate the perspective from which the events and personalities are to be viewed. It is an epical drama, and the Chorus begs to be excused for the inadequacy of the stage for representation of material that is complex, vast, and majestic. But it is a personal, and not a national epic, for the English King fights for his own claims to the throne of France, and the soldiers are inspired more by loyalty to the King than by a national idea, as the Bastard and his men are in *King John*. Henry is the mirror of Christian kings; yet when he is out on a military adventure, he assumes the port of Mars, and his heroism is infectious, for when he visits his soldiers on the eve of the fateful battle of Agincourt, they have 'A little touch of Harry in the night'. It is the King who gives unity to the play and there is perfect correspondence between character and plot. The episodes follow one another in such a continuous stream, and the King's influence is so emphatically underlined in every part of the story, that in spite of all the liberties taken with time and space and in spite of the fact that the historical narrative covers a period of ten years with the scene of action alternating between England and France, the structure is taut rather than loose; and although the centre of the drama is, in violation of Aristotelian principles, a single man rather than a single action, all the parts of the plot may easily be taken in in one view.

There is a good deal of controversy about the character of the protagonist as he emerges from the play. Dover Wilson lists the English contestants in this debate as belonging to two opposed camps: *contra* and *pro*. In the former are Hazlitt, Swinburne, Yeats, Bradley, Masefield, Granville-Barker, Mark Van Doren, and Palmer; and in the latter are Hudson, Dowden, Raleigh, Evans, Bailey, Charles Williams – and Dover Wilson himself.[2] Possibly no character in Shakespeare has so divided the critics as this king who has been hailed as the ideal man of action, the embodiment

---

[1] Introduction to *Henry V* (London Shakespeare, 1958), p. 1018. Munro's Introductions give useful summaries of Shakespearian criticism.

[2] Introduction to *Henry V* (New Cambridge Shakespeare, 1947), p. xv.

of the concept of Heroism, and who has also been condemned as
a self-centred prig with a commonplace mind and a veneer of
piety that only imperfectly covers his craftiness. An analysis of the
play will show that the conflicting estimates of the King's character
are equally true, and they are true because he is a man of action
who is uncritical about his own assumptions. In *Henry IV*, one of
the predominant impressions was his lack of sympathy; he fought
Hotspur but only dimly understood Hotspur's devotion to
chivalry, and mixed with Falstaff but misled the latter about his
own intentions. In *Henry V* his capacity for heroic action is more
in evidence than in *Henry IV*, where he fought only rebels who
were eccentrics and not even united among themselves. Now he is
in a foreign land, toiling against unfavourable conditions and
vastly outnumbered by an enemy in perfect trim. He is heroic
but pious, stern yet merciful, and intrepid and resolute beyond
comparison. But he seldom analyses the basis of his claims or the
subtler implications of his conduct. Even if there are on rare
occasions glimmerings of a deeper sense, he stops short and like
a man of action not of thought, hurries to the work that lies
ready to hand.

By a slight modification of his source, Shakespeare throws light
on the character of the new King and his relationship with the
men on whose support he relies in his French adventure. Shakespeare's Henry is not a mere instrument in the hands of Church
dignitaries, nor is the consultation with the Bishops intended
only to varnish a project which he resolved on much earlier. In
Holinshed the clergy are represented as very much upset by the
proposed bill for the expropriation of church property and they
try to move the King's mind with some sharp invention:

'Whereupon, on a daie in the parliament Henrie Chichelie archbishop
of Canterburie made a pithie oration, wherein he declared how not
onelie the duchies of Normandie and Aquitaine, with the countries of
Anjou and Maine, and the countrie of Gascoigne, were by undoubted
title apperteining to the king, as to the lawfull and onelie heire of the
same, but also the whole realme of France, as heire to his great grandfather king Edward the third.'[1]

Shakespeare divides the two claims – the right of succession to
certain dukedoms, which he put forward before his meeting

---

[1] *Chronicles*, Vol. III, p. 65.

with the Archbishop,[1] and the title to the whole kingdom of France, which he asserted after the exposition of the Salique law in Parliament. Both the claims had been advanced in the right of Edward III, but there was a difference. By the Treaty of Bretigny (1360), Edward III got the Duchy of Aquitaine, the County of Ponthieu, and Calais, but he gave up all claim to the throne of France and to the Plantagenet dominions of Normandy, Maine, and Anjou. But by the Treaty of Bruges (1375), and subsequently by the truce made by Richard II, England lost all her French possessions, except Calais in the north and Bayonne and Bourdeaux in the south. Although Shakespeare was a dramatist and not a historian, the modifications made by him are in accord with history. In this play, Henry V claims at first certain dukedoms in the right of Edward III – obviously those that were ceded by the Treaty of Bretigny – and then after consultation with the nobility and the clergy re-asserts an English King's title to the French throne. In a sense such consultation is unnecessary, because, as Bradley points out, he must know that the Archbishop *wants* war;[2] what is more interesting is that when he speaks to the French ambassador he makes no mention of the Salique law. It is clear that he has made up his mind, and it is characteristic of him that he does not enter into the complex issues involved; but as an efficient general and administrator, he knows that he must have the support of the peers and the clergy, who are the 'noble sinews of (his) power'. The Archbishop's oration helps him to satisfy his conscience that his cause is right, although critics may carp at the way in which it is satisfied; moreover the oration helps to win for him the assistance of his people, so that every man may

> now task his thought,
> That this fair action may on foot be brought.
>
> (l. ii. 309–10)

The King is clever, alert, and able to take firm and quick decision, but his mind is singularly unanalytical. He does not delve into the motives that weigh with the Archbishop, nor does he stop to consider that Edward III, in whose right he is making his demands,

---

[1]*First Amb.*
> Your highness, lately sending into France,
> Did claim some certain dukedoms, in the right
> Of your great predecessor, King Edward the Third.
>   (*Henry V*, I. ii. 246–8)

[2]*Oxford Lectures on Poetry* (London, 1955), p. 257.

himself surrendered the claim to the French throne by the Treaty of Bretigny. If in his discussion with the French ambassadors he does not refer to the Salique law, it is possibly because the French ambassadors might inconveniently point out that even if the English view of the case be accepted and the kingdom can pass to a woman, then, too, Edward III's title would be invalid, for all the brothers of Queen Isabella, Edward III's mother, had daughters. If succession could be claimed through a woman, then Henry V's own right to the English throne would be insecure, for Edmund Mortimer, the descendant of Philippa, daughter to Edward III's third son, would have a better title than Henry V, grandson of John of Gaunt, the fourth son. The Mortimer claim runs like a thread through the three parts of *Henry VI*; it is vigorously pressed by the rebels in I *Henry IV*, but King Henry V seems to be strangely unaware of it. This unawareness becomes dramatically significant when we consider the very elaborate comment made by Holinshed on the punishment given to the Earl of Cambridge and his associates, which is the theme of Act II, sc. i. of *Henry V*:

'This doone, the king thought that surelie all treason and conspiracie had been utterlie extinct: not suspecting the fire which was newlie kindled, and ceased not to increase, till at length it burst out into such a flame, that catching the beames of his house and familie, his line and stocke was cleane consumed to ashes. Diverse write that Richard earle of Cambridge did not conspire with the lord Scroope & Thomas Graie for the murthering of King Henrie to please the French king withall, but onelie to the intent to exalt to the crowne his brother in law Edmund earle of March as heire to Lionell duke of Clarence: after the death of which earle of March, for diverse secret impediments, not able to have issue, the earle of Cambridge was sure that the crowne should come to him by his wife, and to his children, of hir begotten.'[1]

In Shakespeare's play, the Earl of Cambridge does come near to revealing his deep-seated purpose when he says:

> For me, the gold of France did not seduce,
> Although I did admit it as a motive
> The sooner to effect what I intended:
>
> (II. ii. 155–7)

It is characteristic of the King's uncritical attitude that he allows the matter to rest there, and does not pause to ponder what the Earl's real motive might be.

---

[1] *Chronicles*, Vol. III, p. 71.

When Henry V lands in France, he proves, indeed, a valiant general and an exceptionally gifted administrator. The French war is described in two stages – there is the siege of Harfleur in Act III and the decisive victory of Agincourt in Act IV. In the former Henry displays unflinching courage, stern determination, and a capacity for inspiring his people. In peace the principal virtues are stillness and humility,

> But when the blast of war blows in our ears,
> Then imitate the action of the tiger;
> Stiffen the sinews, summon up the blood,
> Disguise fair nature with hard-favour'd rage;
>
> (III. i. 5–8)

He appeals to his soldiers as to 'dear friends', asking them to take their appropriate part in the game which is afoot. He is a refreshing contrast to the French lords – King, Dauphin, and others – who even after their failure to relieve Harfleur and to stop Henry's advance, seriously demand what willing ransom Henry will give and indulge in idle talk of their horses and armour. Shakespeare does not mention two of the factors which explain the French debacle – the state of France which was falling into ruin because of the King's madness and the internal divisions in its politics, and the superior military tactics of the English. The anonymous play– *The Famous Victories of Henry The Fifth* – which Shakespeare used as a source thus describes one of the principal devices by which the English routed the French forces:

> Then I wil, that every archer provide him a stake of
> A tree, and sharpe it at both endes,
> And at the first encounter of the horsemen,
> To pitch their stakes downe in the ground before them,
> That they may gore themselves upon them,
> And then to recoyle backe, and shoote wholly altogither,
> And so discomfit them.[1]

In order to glorify the King and to heighten the effect of the 'little touch of Harry' that inspires his soldiers Shakespeare leaves out important details that accounted for the signal victory of the English. The result is not an unmixed advantage, for although the King looms large with his loftiness and his expansiveness, there is no real conflict, his victory is like a walk-over, and history is transformed into a fairy tale.

---

[1] *Shak. Lib.*, op. cit., p. 363.

The unity of *Henry V* is the unity of the personality of the hero. He is not a 'patchwork' figure, but a homogeneous character in whom disparate traits are inextricably intermingled. He is at the van of the army, shares all its discomforts, and although no democrat mixes with the commonest soldier as with a brother:

> We few, we happy few, we band of brothers;
> For he to-day that sheds his blood with me
> Shall be my brother;
>
> (IV. iii. 60–62)

As pointed out before, the centre of the epic is not the country but the King. There is some truth in the suggestion that through the portraiture of Henry V Shakespeare becomes a prophetic harbinger of the union of different peoples – Englishmen as well as Irishmen and Scotsmen and Welshmen – but the important point is that the men serve the King rather than the cause of England. Indeed, Fluellen flaunts his Welsh nationality with an extravagance that is half-comical, and the Irish Mac Morris is so sensitive on the subject of his nationality that the slightest reflection on it would make him rush at the throat of the slanderer:

> Of my nation! What ish my nation? ish a villain, and a bastard, and a knave, and a rascal? What ish my nation? Who talks of my nation?
>
> (III. ii. 136–9)

The defiance is so fierce that even the sturdy Fluellen is eager for a compromise. Yet sensitive as the Irishman is, he is passionately devoted to the King, and in the siege of Harfleur, the Duke of Gloucester, the King's brother, is 'altogether directed' by him. The more voluble Fluellen who is attached equally deeply to the King makes a compromise between his loyalty and his nationalism by claiming that Henry V himself is a Welshman:

> All the water in Wye cannot wash your majesty's Welsh plood out of your pody, I can tell you that: Got bless it and preserve it, as long as it pleases his grace, and his majesty too!
>
> (IV. vii. 112–15)

Henry V's religion and morality are of a piece with his other characteristics. Although he exhorts his soldiers to imitate the action of the tiger, he tempers his fury with mercy. He holds out terrible threats to the Governor of Harfleur, and we have no reason to think that these are empty threats, but as soon as the Governor yields the town his instruction is: Use mercy to them all. And later on he gives charge that nothing be taken but paid for and the French be not upbraided or abused in disdainful language. But his mercy is less the emanation of an instinct of charity than the result of cold calculation, for he knows that when 'lenity and cruelty play for a kingdom, the gentler gamester is the soonest winner' (III. vi. 121–3). His subsequent direction that every English soldier kill his prisoner need not cause any surprise. Although victorious, he is vastly outnumbered in a foreign country and he cannot take any risk. Even though the French have been routed, they seem to be making new preparations and to be loath to 'void the field'. Besides, the runaway French soldiers have made a cowardly attack on the luggage, killing the boys who were in charge of it. In Fluellen's opinion, such an attack is 'expressly against the law of arms', and Gower goes so far as to say that this cruel act makes Henry a gallant king. But the order is neither cruel nor gallant; it only shows that he is 'in his right wits and good judgments' and doing just what the situation requires. It is because his moral sense is the servant of his policy that he is sometimes priggish and extravagant, but although the hero of a historical drama which merges into a fairy tale, he is at heart a realist who knows that 'nice customs curtsy to great kings' but also that what we call the majesty or glory of kingship is little better than ceremony. It is the same thing with his emotions. He is fascinated by the French Princess whom he woos in his rough soldierly manner, but it is doubtful if he would have been so fascinated if this marriage did not end the French war and give him the right of succession to the French throne.

There is no reason to doubt the sincerity of his piety, his gratitude to God for the victory he has won. But his piety is uncritical, and as Bradley points out, 'also superstitious – an attempt to buy off supernatural vengeance for Richard's blood; and it is also in part political, like his father's projected crusade'.[1] We may contrast his piety with that of Claudius, who is in a worse spiritual state, because he is a real criminal, whereas Henry only enjoys the fruits of a crime committed by his father. The genuineness of Claudius's repentance is proved by his realization that it cannot be genuine:

> O! What form of prayer
> Can serve my turn? 'Forgive me my foul murder'?

---

[1] op. ci ., p. 257

That cannot be; since I am still possess'd
Of those effects for which I did the murder,
My crown, mine own ambition, and my queen.
May one be pardon'd and retain the offence?

(Hamlet, III. iii. 51–56)*

This may be compared with Henry's appeal to God on the eve of the Battle of Agincourt:

Not to-day, O Lord!
O! not to-day, think not upon the fault
My father made in compassing the crown.
I Richard's body have interr'd anew,
And on it have bestow'd more contrite tears
Than from it issu'd forced drops of blood.
Five hundred poor I have in yearly pay,
Who twice a day their wither'd hands hold up
Towards heaven, to pardon blood; and I have built
Two chantries, where the sad and solemn priests
Sing still for Richard's soul. More will I do;
Though all that I can do is nothing worth,
Since that my penitence comes after all,
Imploring pardon.

(Henry V, IV. i. 312–25)*

It is worth noticing that he gives an elaborate description of the ritual of piety, but when it comes to the crucial question whether such penitence as his can have any value he tails off abruptly; his thinking is confused and his expression halting. His prayer has not the depth or poignancy of Claudius's repentance. He does not stop to examine whether it is right for him to enjoy the fruits of his father's fault or whether even if Heaven may 'pardon blood', the crown should not be surrendered to the Mortimer line. His mind is active and alert, but it is insufficiently critical and unwilling to pursue the subtlest implications of its own thought.

His mental limitations are more glaringly brought to light when at night, in the disguise of an ordinary soldier, he meets John Bates, Alexander Court, and Michael Williams. His long association with Falstaff and his crew has not corrupted his mind, but it has made him a good mixer; he can move amongst common soldiers as if he were one of them. Wide experience of the various strata of society has given him an intimate knowledge of men and things – of the unyoked humour of the Corinthians as also of the ceremonies that surround kings, although 'all (their) senses have but human conditions'. He inspires unflinching loyalty in his followers, but when he has to convince them about the justness of his cause, he only shows how 'weak' his thinking is. The sturdy Williams says that many soldiers will die in the impending battle, 'some swearing, some crying for a surgeon, some upon their wives left poor behind them, some upon the debts they owe, some upon their children rawly left'. He is afraid that few of those that die in a battle, die well; here, particularly, he does not know whether the King for whom they are fighting has a just cause and an honourable quarrel. The King delivers a long sermon, but he dodges the issue and succeeds only in deceiving Bates and Williams – and possibly himself. By a verbal quibble, he dwells only on one meaning of 'dying well', and placidly concludes that no king is answerable for the personal sins of his soldiers:

> 'So, if a son that is by his father sent about merchandise do sinfully miscarry upon the sea, the imputation of his wickedness, by your rule, should be imposed upon his father that sent him: or if a servant, under his master's command transporting a sum of money, be assailed by robbers and die in many irreconciled iniquities, you may call the business of the master the author of the servant's damnation.'
>
> (IV. i. 156–64)

Both the analogies are fallacious. It is not the son's sinfulness but the rightness of the father's business that is in dispute. In the second analogy, the King assumes the truth of what he pretends to prove, namely, that the assailing (or defending?) Frenchmen are robbers. He has no answer – and does not seem to know that he has no answer – to the suggestion made by Williams and Bates, that if his cause is not good he is morally culpable for sending his men to death, and their obedience to him wipes off their responsibility for taking part in an unjust war. Henry V's reasoning here is quite in line with his earlier actions. He never stopped to enquire whether in concealing his ulterior purpose he was quite fair to Falstaff. He sent ambassadors to France, claiming certain dukedoms – to be followed by a larger claim – before he had consulted the Archbishop of Canterbury. Later on he adjures the Archbishop to ponder the matter seriously, because on his advice will depend the fates of thousands of men, but he does not relate the Primate's advice to the bill for the confiscation of Church temporalties, nor does he care to enquire whether, if the

Salique law is inoperative, he has a right to the throne he is occupying.

Henry V is, indeed, a creation of the 'complaisant' side of Shakespeare's genius. But there is also the 'daemonic', critical side of which we get glimpses in the doubts raised by Williams and Bates, who are silenced but whose questions remain unanswered.[1] The deeper undertones of Shakespeare's meaning are most eloquently expressed in this play in the touching description of Falstaff's death; although written in prose, it is one of the most poetical passages in the whole range of Shakespeare's work. It shows what a profound effect the Rejection at the end of 2 *Henry IV* had on his imagination. This brings us to another question hotly debated by critics – the dramatic appropriateness of the comic scenes in *Henry V*. If Shakespeare did not want to continue the story of Hal in France with Sir John in it, should he not have left him and his straggling followers out of it altogether? Or, did he, consistently with the promise made in the Epilogue to 2 *Henry IV*, introduce the fat knight in a first draft and then on the retirement of Kempe, who played Falstaff, from the Chamberlain's Company, write the scene of Falstaff's death, substituting Pistol for Falstaff in the ordeal of the leek? This seems to be an ingenious but far-fetched view, for there is nothing casual in the comic scenes which are organically connected with the substance of the play, and there is no evidence or ground for thinking that the description of Falstaff's death is an after-thought. The play of *Henry V* gives the best justification for the rejection of Falstaff; it gives a lurid picture of the activities of Falstaff's company when Falstaff's own genius is not there to cast its halo upon them. Nym, Bardolph, and Pistol are 'swashers' and sworn brothers in filching, incapable of noble thought or action, and absolutely untouched by the heroic idealism with which the rest of the army is inspired. The Prince could tolerate them when he was unburdened with responsibilities; but when he has serious business on hand, they have no place in his government or his army. Nym and Bardolph are hanged, and although Fluellen makes an appeal for mercy on behalf of Bardolph, no one pays any heed to such an appeal. They are rightly served, and Pistol, from whose weary limbs honour is

---

[1]Clifford Leech, writing about 2 *Henry IV*, puts forward this view cautiously but trenchantly: 'We do him, I think, scant justice if we assume that he could write complacently of Prince John of Lancaster and could have no doubts about Prince Hal'. (*Shakespeare Survey*, Vol. 6, p. 24.)

cudgelled, hurries back to England to take up the profession of a bawd and a cutpurse. It is when we look at them away from their leader that we realize how disgusting they are socially, and then we understand the truth of Fluellen's assertion that 'Harry of Monmouth, being in his right wits and his good judgments, turned away the fat knight with the great belly-doublet' (IV. vii. 50–52).

But 'right wits and good judgments' are not the whole of life. In turning away the fat knight Harry of Monmouth turned his back on the world of beauty and joy, of flowers and green fields, of all-hallown summer and latter spring. In representing Falstaff's end Shakespeare skims lightly over his principal vices – his addiction to wine and to women – and creates a scene of pure beauty and pathos, of how at the turning of the tide, with his heart fracted and corroborate, he passes out of an unkind world safely into Arthur's (or Abraham's) bosom if ever any man went there.

CHAPTER SIX

Henry VIII

I

ALTHOUGH after *Henry V* (1599), Shakespeare turned away
from the writing of historical plays, he did not forget Holinshed,
for of the great tragedies, *King Lear* and *Macbeth*, and of the final
romances, *Cymbeline*, are all chronicle stories. As these plays refer
to very remote times, and *Macbeth* has little to do with England,
they are not true 'histories'. The romances mark the end of
Shakespeare's dramatic career, and Prospero's burying his magic
wand is said to symbolize Shakespeare's retirement from dramatic
workmanship as player and playwright. But it seems that even
after this retirement signalized by *The Tempest* (1610–11), Shakespeare returned to the writing of plays and wrote *Henry VIII*
(1612–13), and possibly collaborated in the composition of *The
Two Noble Kinsmen* – and the lost *Cardenio*. *Henry VIII*, if it is entirely
Shakespeare's work, which many have doubted, is remarkable
for a variety of reasons. It marks a return to English history which
Shakespeare left far behind him, and the history it represents is
not of far off days but of men and things very near Shakespeare's
time, and thus touches on live political and religious issues. In
tone and temper this play is different from Shakespeare's other
histories; it has been described as a splendid spectacle more akin
to the final romances than to the plays written in the early and
middle periods of his career. Indeed, the Prologue to *Henry VIII*
indicates the difference between this and the other historical
plays:

> Only they
> That come to hear a merry, bawdy play,
> A noise of targets, or to see a fellow
> In a long motley coat guarded with yellow,
> Will be deceiv'd; for, gentle hearers, know,
> To rank our chosen truth with such a show

As fool and fight is, besides forfeiting
Our own brains, and the opinion that we bring,
To make that only true we now intend,
Will leave us never an understanding friend.
Therefore for goodness' sake, and as you are known
The first and happiest hearers of the town,
Be sad, as we should make ye: think ye see
The very persons of our noble story
As they were living; think you see them great,
And follow'd with the general throng and sweat
Of thousand friends; then, in a moment see
How soon this mightiness meets misery:
And if you can be merry then, I'll say
A man may weep upon his wedding day.

The general critical opinion is that these lines refer to Rowley's farcical historical fantasy *When you see me, You know me*, which was published in 1605. Although the immediate reference may be to Rowley's play, the criticism made here can be extended to chronicle narratives like *Henry IV* and *Henry V*, which are merry bawdy plays with plentiful noise of targets. *Henry VIII* is not without its share of foolery but there is no fighting, which is so abundant in Shakespeare's other historical plays.

The change of emphasis may be illustrated by means of a comparison between the Prologues of *Henry V* and *Henry VIII*. In the former, Shakespeare seems to be impressed by the vastness of his martial theme and only anxious about whether the stage will be able to render it. In *Henry VIII*, it is not the vastness of his subject but its truth and its melancholy moral that engage the poet's attention. Is the drama then a variation on the old medieval theme of the Fall of Princes, of how mightiness meets misery? That this subject was uppermost in Shakespeare's mind is shown by the most important episodes in the drama – of Buckingham, Wolsey, and Queen Katharine. But in Shakespeare's works it is not where he starts but how he ends that is of primary importance. He might have taken as his theme the falls of these great personages with the intention of making it a sad story, but the drama ends on a note of triumph and not of tragedy. It records the fall of Wolsey and Katharine but also celebrates the ascendancy of Cranmer and Anne Bullen, and since no reference is made to the disasters which overtook these personages, it cannot be said that the final impression is tragic or that the play is a kind of morality on the theme of the fickleness of Fortune. *Henry VIII* is a true 'history' not merely because it follows the chronicles, but also because in tone and temper it steers a middle course between the light-heartedness – the merry bawdiness – of comedy and the gloom of tragedy.

If *Henry VIII* is placed in the context of the other historical plays of Shakespeare, its most striking feature seems to be the novelty of its political and social atmosphere. In the plays dealing with the Middle Ages, the King, even when powerful, depended very much on the support of the nobility and the clergy. But in *Henry VIII*, we are in a world that is definitely modern. Here the king is supreme, the noblemen have sunk into the background, and a new generation of ministers and advisers – drawn from the humblest ranks – have come to the forefront. Not only does the butcher's son Wolsey make the chief peer of the realm lessen his big look but the King's Council with a majority of peers is powerless against Cranmer, a priest very much unlike the overbearing Wolsey, but, equally with Wolsey, a man of undistinguished social antecedents. The Duke of Buckingham derives some consolation from the fact that he was given a trial before being condemned – a noble one in the sense that it was held by his peers – whereas his wretched father was summarily beheaded. The father, however, was a mighty man of whom King Richard was afraid as one who had helped him to the throne and might try to uncrown him, whereas the son is only an ordinary traitor whom the King orders to be taken through the usual process of law, which is but a show managed by the wily Wolsey whom Buckingham is unable to resist:

> This butcher's cur is venom-mouth'd, and I
> Have not the power to muzzle him; therefore best
> Not wake him in his slumber. A beggar's book
> Outworths a noble's blood.
>
> (I. i. 120–3)

The comparison suggested previously between *Henry V* and *Henry VIII* may be further elaborated, because the difference is between the medieval world dominated by barons and the Tudor world of absolute monarchy. In *Henry V*, the King seeks foreign quarrels partly because this would, as his father said, busy the giddy minds of the lords who might otherwise be a source of trouble in times of peace, and the Epilogue shows that this experiment brings only a temporary lull in the squabbles of the

warring lords and that before long not only will France be lost
but England will be made to bleed. In *Henry VIII*, there is talk of
foreign alliances, but not of foreign wars, and ambitious and
arrogant men are entirely subservient to the King's will. The
King's position and authority are unassailable; he does not plan
everything in advance as does Prospero in *The Tempest*, but he can
control men and things with almost God-like omnipotence.

The incident which marked the acme of Henry's ascendancy
was both a personal affair and a sign-post in the evolution of modern
England. This was his breach with Rome, which had far-reaching
repercussions in national politics and religion and also in international relations. But it had its roots in a personal problem: Was
Henry legally married to Queen Katharine with whom he had
lived happily for more than twenty years? In tracing the intricacy
of this problem which was charged with such momentous consequences, Shakespeare, as is his wont, lays emphasis on its purely
human aspects, and though he only half succeeds in unravelling
the tangled web, the attempt itself is characteristic of his genius.
One of the puzzling questions in English history is: When did
Henry VIII fall in love with Anne Bullen and what effect had this
passion on his conscientious scruples about the validity of his
marriage with Katharine? In history – that is to say, in Hall and
Holinshed – these two affairs lie apart, though the scruples about
the marriage are so quickly followed by rumours about the liaison
that it seems strange that these historians do not try to interrelate
them; and modern writers have asked if the foundation stone of
the Anglican Church was not an amatory intrigue of Henry VIII.
The question about the Queen's marriage was raised when, at the
instigation of Wolsey, Henry decided on forsaking the Emperor,
the nephew of Katharine, and on embarking on an alliance with
France. Then the proposal was made that Princess Mary, Henry
and Katharine's daughter, be betrothed to a son of the French
King. Suddenly rumours were afloat, casting suspicion about the
legitimacy of the Princess, and even a marriage with the Duchess
of Alençon, the French King's sister, was proposed for Henry.
Since Wolsey was the engineer of the French alliance and regarded as hostile to the Queen, he might have started the mischief, though both he and King Henry repudiated the suggestion.
But as the proceedings for divorcing Queen Katharine were taken
up, news of the King's setting his affections on Anne Bullen
leaked out and Queen Katharine became an object of everybody's

sympathy, not excluding Anne Bullen's in Shakespeare's play. It is a matter of speculation whether the King's conscience had been troubled only because it had, as Suffolk suggests here, crept too near another lady or whether the King had not been crossed by doubts much earlier than his meeting with Anne. There is evidence that as far back as 1514 Henry thought of repudiating Katharine, but this is not mentioned by either Hall or Holinshed.

In the chronicles, the two motives for Henry's action have little connexion with each other, for the chroniclers are primarily interested to show how this affair affected Wolsey's fortunes and – though somewhat distantly – the national and international situation. With a boldness characteristic of his imagination, Shakespeare mixes the two themes by making the love affair between Henry and Anne start much earlier than it did in fact. Buckingham was executed in 1521, the question of the divorce was not 'bruited' before 1527 and Henry did not marry Anne till towards the end of 1532 (or in January 1533). But Shakespeare makes Henry court Anne even before the condemnation of Buckingham, when, historically, she would be less than fifteen; and almost immediately after the execution of the Duke there is a 'buzzing' of a separation between Henry and his Queen. What is the cause of this 'ensuing evil'? Is it due entirely to the machinations of Cardinal Wolsey who wants to have Katharine put away? For all that we know, the King's doubts are genuine, and it is a hard wrench for him to part from his wife. But the Duke of Suffolk has already suggested that the King's conscience has been activated by his fondness for another lady. In Act II. sc. iii, the Old Lady, whom we meet in the company of Anne, only confirms Suffolk's insinuation and prophesies that she will soon venture to be a queen for all England. Anne herself, though young and apparently unambitious, has her own intuitions. The announcement that she has been made Marchioness of Pembroke with a thousand pounds a year causes her more trembling and bewilderment than pleasure:

> Would I had no being,
> If this salute my blood a jot; it faints me,
> To think what follows.
> The queen is comfortless, and we forgetful
> In our long absence. Pray, do not deliver
> What you've heard to her.
>
> (II. iii. 102–07)

In Shakespeare's version, Anne Bullen exercises a much greater influence on the course of events than is warranted by Hall's account or Holinshed's. In the chronicle narrative, the King's wrath is aroused only when the Cardinals have dissolved the Court and Cardinal Campeius has expressed a desire to refer the whole matter to the Pope.[1] In *Henry VIII*, they adjourn the proceedings until they have been able to persuade the Queen to revoke her appeal to Rome, and the King forthwith exclaims in an aside:

> I may perceive
> These cardinals trifle with me: I abhor
> This dilatory sloth and tricks of Rome,
>
> (II. iv. 233–5)

which shows that since his mind is made up, the reference to the Cardinals was an unnecessary formality, and all this is due to the fascination Anne Bullen has exercised on him. But the King is genuinely fond of his wife Katharine, his sweet bed-fellow for twenty years, and it is significant that Katharine's complaint is largely against Wolsey and only partly against the King; she never mentions Anne, one of the ladies in her own court. The two impulses in the King's heart seem to exist side by side; they do not attract and interpenetrate each other and produce a tragic tension. The attempt at the mingling of different forces is charac-teristic of Shakespeare's genius, but there is not that fusion which we find in his heroes and heroines in the mature comedies, and more particularly in the great tragedies.

If from Henry VIII we turn to the butcher's son, who according to Pater helps to define the central interest of the play, we have the same feeling of incompleteness.[2] Both Hall and Holinshed portray Wolsey as crafty, ambitious, and arrogant, and both of them present him as exercising an undue influence on the King till the matter of the divorce drives a wedge between the two, though we find that at least on one occasion the King reproved him sharply, saying that 'yet it were long he would look to things

---

[1]Hall: op. cit., p. 758. The Cardinal does not here openly express his desire, but Henry is shrewd enough to see through the game. Holinshed, *Chronicles*, III, pp. 739–40.

In Holinshed the King's suspicion is aroused before the reference to the Pope, but only when he finds the Cardinals making unnecessary delay: '. . . he openly perceived that the Legats dissimuled the tyme to have the matter in the courte of Rome . . .'.

[2]*Appreciations*, p. 187.

himselfe without anie substitut'.[1] In Shakespeare's portrait which is based on Hall and Holinshed, the Cardinal's influence, prior to the Black-Friars Trial, is even more pervasive than in the sources, and more inexplicable, for we have only very faint glimpses of Wolsey's grandiose schemes and labyrinthine diplomacy. Modern historians, surveying the age of Henry VIII without the near-contemporary bias that obscured the vision of Elizabethan writers, have realized the true nature of Wolsey's ascendancy over Henry VIII. The immediate results of his policies were confused, and his lavishness on such projects as the meeting on The Field of the Cloth of Gold might appear to men like Buckingham to be wasteful. But by tearing away England from the Holy League, by winning the friendship of France and by playing off – as occasions arose – France against Spain, Wolsey helped to give England a decisive role in international diplomacy. All this was obscure to Hall, Holinshed, Cavendish – and to Shakespeare. The defect of Shakespeare's portraiture, however, is not that he lacked the knowledge or insight to place Wolsey's diplomatic schemes in their proper historical perspective, but that here he cannot delve into what Lamb felicitously describes as 'the inner structure and workings of mind in a character'.[2]

Wolsey claims – in the play as well as in history – that he was a devoted servant of the King and if he had served God with half the zeal with which he served his King, God would not in his age have left him naked to his enemies. But it does not appear how he served King Henry and how this devotion was woven into his personal ambition. He sends Buckingham to the block, but that is because Buckingham is his personal enemy rather than a man dangerous to the state. In the play, although Queen Katharine is bitterly opposed to him, it is not clear whether it is he who has aroused scruples in the King's mind about the validity of his marriage, or indeed whether he seriously wants to have the marriage annulled. There is a suggestion that he might have tried to revenge himself on the Spanish King for his failure to get the Archbishopric of Toledo, but it is no more than a suggestion. He makes an appeal to the Pope to stay judgement in the divorce proceedings, which is a move in Katharine's favour, and here his motives are a firm dislike of Anne Bullen and jealousy of the growing power of Cranmer:

---

[1] Holinshed, *Chronicles*, III, p. 685.
[2] *English Critical Essays* (Nineteenth Century, W.C. 206), p. 85.

> Yet I know her for
> A spleeny Lutheran; and not wholesome to
> Our cause, that she should lie i' the bosom of
> Our hard-rul'd king. Again there is sprung up
> A heretic, an arch one, Cranmer; one
> Hath crawl'd into the favour of the king,
> And is his oracle.
>
> (III. ii. 99–105)

What is 'our cause'? Is it his own power and position? Or is it the cause of the old religion? Or the King's larger interests? What grounds has he so far for thinking that the King is hard to rule and may pass under the influence of an attractive Lutheran? The comments made in the above speech are derived from the chronicle account which Shakespeare merely puts into vigorous verse. But description is one thing and dramatic portraiture another. The Duke of Norfolk speaks of his 'contrary proceedings' in the matter of the divorce (III. ii. 26); the proceedings are 'contrary' in more senses than one, because they contradict the King's wishes as much as they contradict themselves. We have only vague ideas of Wolsey's mazy schemes, and look in vain for the inner self lying behind these schemes and his immediate surface motives. While he was alive, he was feared and hated by all classes of people and had only one faithful follower in Cromwell. After his death Griffith speaks of him as extraordinarily ambitious, but also as 'Exceeding wise, fair-spoken and persuading'. But in the scenes in which he appears, he is seldom fair-spoken, there is no evidence of exceeding wisdom and very little of persuasiveness. He seemed to exercise a kind of witchcraft over the King, but in the affair of the divorce, his 'spell in that is out'. What reactions the sudden discovery of the King's intractability arouses in him and how it is reflected in his thought and conduct is not revealed in the drama from which he retires in a blaze of rhetoric. His speech bidding farewell to all his greatness is magnificent, but it is declamatory rather than dramatic, for it is not fused with his other thoughts, emotions, and ideas; he seems to contemplate his fall like a spectator. A plaything of Fortune, he does not come fully to life as a dramatic character.

Queen Katharine shares with Cardinal Wolsey the distinction of being the protagonist of the play which is named after neither of them. The Queen's part has been the favourite of great actresses, and Dr Johnson's opinion – 'The genius of Shakespeare comes in and goes out with Katharine'[1] – although an exaggeration, has an element of truth. Shakespeare bases his account of her misfortune on Holinshed's *Chronicles*, in which she is presented as a loving, submissive wife but firm in her opposition to Wolsey and unflinching in her decision to lay her cause before the Pope. Shakespeare accepts this view of her character but adds touches of his own which heighten her pathetic attractiveness. She champions the poor people wronged by Wolsey's taxes and sees through his wiles in Buckingham's trial, openly protesting that the evidence produced against the Duke is unreliable. When her own cause is before the Cardinals, her 'drops of tears' are really turned into 'sparks of fire', and she even mocks her formidable enemy when he asks her to be patient, or pedantically addresses her in Latin. Although full of piety and charity, she does not forgive him even in death, and her description of him shows a keen relish of his fall from greatness:

> i' the presence
> He would say untruths, and be ever double
> Both in words and meaning. He was never,
> But where he meant to ruin, pitiful;
> His promises were, as he then was, mighty;
> But his performance, as he now is, nothing:
> Of his own body he was ill, and gave
> The clergy ill example.
>
> (IV. ii. 37–44)

The story of Katharine is told with both delicacy and power, and The Vision of Fairies is an experiment in fantasy in Shakespeare's best manner. But even here there is the same impression of superficiality that is produced by the other episodes and characters. Katharine reacts to every situation swiftly and firmly; even Wolsey who deceives the King cannot deceive her. But she does not know what everyone knows, that her husband is passionately in love with one of her own maids of honour. It is only once that she seems to realize that her problem is not merely religious or political, but personal; it is the tragedy of an ageing woman mated to a man several years younger than her:

> Would ye have me, –
> If ye have any justice, any pity;
> If ye be anything but churchmen's habits, –

---

[1] *Johnson on Shakespeare* (ed. W. Raleigh, London, 1908), p. 152.

M

> Put my sick cause into his hands that hates me?
> Alas! he has banish'd me his bed already,
> His love, too long ago! I am old, my lords,
> And all the fellowship I hold now with him
> Is only my obedience.
>
> (III. i. 114–21)

It is only on this single occasion that she comes near probing what was possibly the saddest point in her tragedy, but even here she does not mention how her husband has been tangled in the affections of a younger rival.

The episode of Katharine fails to reach the heights of dramatic poetry for yet another reason. Mere passive suffering does not bring the whole soul of man into activity, and is, as Matthew Arnold points out, an unsuitable subject for poetry. We cannot derive poetical enjoyment from subjects in which 'the suffering finds no vent in action; in which a continuous state of mental distress is prolonged, unrelieved by incident, hope, or resistance, in which there is everything to be endured, nothing to be done'.[1] Beyond making an appeal to Rome and persisting in her refusal to withdraw the appeal she does little that is of any significance. She feels the loss of her position as wife and queen and resents the new style in which people are expected to address her now, but otherwise she submits calmly and pines away to death. History does not assign to her any other role, and it is true that outwardly she could do little. But the dramatist cannot reveal the inner life where her thoughts and emotions clashed and coalesced and she was something more than a passive sufferer.

II

One reason why the various episodes of *Henry VIII* produce an impression of superficiality is that there is no concentration on any particular action, and the drama seems to be without any central purpose. Henry VIII himself seems to stand outside the drama, although it is named after him and he emerges to impose his will at every stage. Without his approval Buckingham could not have been condemned to death; it is he who dismisses Wolsey, divorces Katharine, and saves Cranmer. Still, Buckingham, Wolsey, Katharine, and Cranmer, are in the foreground; the drama is their story rather than his. But although the beheading of Buckingham

---

[1] Preface to *Poems*, 1853 (W.C. No. 206), p. 306.

removes a friend who might have helped Katharine in her hour of need, he has nothing to do with her in the play, and she only shows ineffective sympathy for him. Henry's learned and well-beloved servant Cranmer is said to bring comfort to his master, but how he does it remains obscure, and Katharine, who is so critical of Wolsey, never says a word about the priest who plays the most decisive part in annulling her marriage. Wolsey has, indeed, a finger in every pie, but he does not appear in the last two acts at all. The most heroic person in the earlier stages of the play is Katharine who suffers undeservedly, but the later scenes are a glorification of her supplanter Anne Bullen. 'The scheme of *Henry VIII*', as Dowden observes – and many critics agree with him – 'has no dramatic centre; no ascent, no culmination, no subsidence. The tragedy of Buckingham is succeeded by the tragedy of Wolsey, and this by the tragedy of Katharine, then the play closes with triumphs and rejoicings. The fifth act, for one who has been deeply interested in the story of the Cardinal and the story of the Queen, is an artistic impertinence'.[1]

This dramatic incoherence or lack of a consistent design started a train of doubts and investigations which were clinched by Spedding and Hickson, who in the middle of the nineteenth century put forward the thesis that the play, which is written in two styles, was the joint work of Fletcher and Shakespeare.[2] Other investigators advanced claims for other dramatists, such as Massinger, but the collaboration of Fletcher was generally accepted. It was confidently asserted that Shakespeare wrote only I. i, ii; II. iii, iv; III. ii. 1–203; V. i; and Fletcher was responsible for the rest of the play. Of the major critics of the nineteenth century Swinburne alone thought it to be entirely by Shakespeare,[3] but in recent times Wilson Knight and Peter Alexander have put forward convincing pleas in favour of Shakespeare's sole author-ship.[4] Wilson Knight, in particular, has shown in the course of a very detailed analysis that the Shakespearian echoes are much stronger than the Fletcherian, and Peter Alexander points out that stylistic characteristics claimed as peculiar to Fletcher are

---

[1]Introduction to *Henry VIII* (Imperial Edition)

[2]Spedding: *Sh. Soc. Trans.* (1874). Much has been made of Hickson and Spedding arriving at the same results independently, but Peter Alexander (*Essays and Studies*, XVI, 1930, p. 103) significantly points out that 'once the test proposed by Hickson was accepted it was merely a matter of counting double-endings. It would have been strange had they not succeeded in counting alike'.

[3]*A Study of Shakespeare* (London, 1880), pp. 81–100.

[4]*The Crown of Life* (London, 1958), pp. 256–72. Alexander, op. cit., pp. 85–120.

also found in Shakespeare.[1] The arguments on both sides have been
usefully summarized by R. A. Foakes, who also supports the
theory of Shakespeare's undivided authorship.[2] but not all would
accept this view. Middleton Murry and Tillyard, for example,
exclude *Henry VIII* from their studies, and A. C. Partridge has
made out a new case for Fletcher's part-authorship.[3]

It will be unnecessary to go over the ground so well traversed
by previous critics, for in such a matter where the ultimate
source of belief is our inner impression it is difficult for one party
to convince another. We have to remember that so far as external
evidence is concerned there is nothing to supersede the testimony
of Heminge and Condell, who published the play for the first time
and published it as a work by Shakespeare, though Fletcher was
alive at the time. There might be a thousand reasons for their
excluding from their collection a play that might have been
written by Shakespeare, but there can be but one reason why
they included a play in it, and that is that they knew and not
merely surmised that this particular work was written solely –
or largely – by Shakespeare. This may look like an over-simplification of the problems of textual and bibliographical criticism, but
no argument is more convincing than the simple fact that Shakespeare's first editors, who were also his friends and fellow-actors,
excluded *The Two Noble Kinsmen* and *Cardenio* but included
Henry VIII. Yet another point for consideration is that the 'disinte-
grators', although they might adduce stylistic evidence in support
of their theory of joint authorship, have first been impelled by a
feeling that it is a relatively poor work which in its inferior
passages must have been written by one of Shakespeare's contemporaries. So they have proceeded from this subjective feeling
to the objective evidence of difference in style. But if we trust
to our feeling, supported by the unchallengeable authority of
Heminge and Condell, it will be difficult to credit Fletcher with
the authorship of many of the scenes attributed to him. Spedding
himself felt that the Fourth Act, which incidentally contains the
scene of Katharine's death, is too vigorous for Fletcher. Nevertheless he and Hickson attributed it to Fletcher. The same thing
may be said of many other scenes, most notably of the second

[1]Alexander, op. cit., p. 106.
[2]Introduction to *Henry VIII* (New Arden Shakespeare, London, 1957), pp. xv–xxvi.
[3]*The Problem of Henry VIII Re-opened* (Bowes and Bowes, Cambridge, 1949). The case
for dual authorship has been vigorously argued also by J. C. Maxwell in the Introduction to
Henry VIII (New Cambridge Shakespeare, 1962).

half of III. ii, containing Wolsey's farewell speeches, which, in spite of their rhetorical exuberance, look indubitably Shakespearian to the ordinary reader or spectator. Swinburne is a brilliant, but not always a reliable critic; yet he echoes our sentiments when at the conclusion of his appreciation of the scene in which Buckingham is led to his execution, he says: 'If indeed Fletcher could have written this scene, or the farewell of Wolsey to his greatness, or his parting scene with Cromwell, he was perhaps not a great poet, but he certainly was a tragic writer capable of loftier self-control and severer self-command, than he has ever shown himself elsewhere.'[1]

One argument which has not received sufficient attention may be stressed here. Although there is an appearance of confusion in the design of the plot, there is none in the characterization, which may be immature but not incoherent. Henry's confronting Wolsey with his own list of his assets and his letter to the Pope is of a piece with his checkmating of Gardiner and other members of the Council with a ring given to Cranmer. If one of these episodes is by Shakespeare, the other should be by him too. The representation of the Anne Bullen tangle furnishes more convincing evidence of this unity of conception, and there are lines unmistakably Shakespearian even in scenes usually assigned to Fletcher. In this play Anne meets and fascinates Henry much earlier than in history, and although the King is depicted neither subtly nor deeply, his decision to leave Katharine at the bidding of his conscience, even before the trial has begun, is a piece of partly unconscious hypocrisy that fits in well with what comes before and after, and is reminiscent of Shakespeare's delineation of other enigmatic situations and characters. The mind that conceived the scene of the Black-Friars Trial (II. iv) must have conceived the scene of the meeting of Katharine and the Bishops (III. i), and the two scenes seem to have been written by the same hand, too. The sympathetic sketch of Anne – the dramatist's most original portraiture in this play – in the early stages of the story is an appropriate prelude to the triumphs and rejoicings in the Fifth Act, although these later scenes might be an artistic impertinence for some readers and spectators who have followed with sympathy the episode of the Cardinal or of Queen Katharine.

---

[1] *A Study of Shakespeare*, p. 86.

III

If *Henry VIII* is to be regarded as a work of undivided authorship, what can its total significance be? Since the plot is only a sequence of private disasters, in the course of which Buckingham, Wolsey, and Katharine are overwhelmed and Cranmer just scrapes through, the deeper import of the play may be sought in some central idea lying outside action and character but projected by them. It has been suggested that one of the dominant themes of the play is the virtue of patience, which all the leading characters learn to practise. The suggestion is plausible, for Buckingham does not think of organizing a rebellion as did his father, Wolsey bears his misfortunes stoically, and Katharine's last wish is to be 'remembered in all humility unto his highness'; indeed, one of her maids is called Patience, and she seems to be an emanation from Katharine rather than an independent character. Though all the victims of royal caprice are endowed with fortitude, yet, the predominant impression is one of helplessness rather than of patience. Katharine till the last moment refuses to surrender her case to the judgement of her husband whom, however, she blesses in death. Buckingham and Wolsey both face their disasters with dignity but they seem to be powerless rather than patient. Even when the axe falls on Buckingham, he protests his innocence, and although he has no malice against the law, he has a fling at those who procured the evidence upon which he was convicted. Wolsey is undone partly by his own folly, and after finding that his letter to the Pope has been seen by the King and there is no way left, he visualizes the magnificence of his fall as that of a bright exhalation in the evening. He does not dwell on the virtue of patience as an antidote to the misfortunes of life. Nor can it be said that the play finds living symbols for the ideals of peace or justice, as has been claimed by some interpreters.[1] Although there is no mention of civil dissension or foreign war, the theme of the earlier histories, the world presented here is so torn with strife, so full of conspiracies and counter-conspiracies that no one seems to be safe and the reins of authority are in the hands of a wayward autocrat whose will is law. Henry VIII has been likened to Prospero, but he does not reconcile or forgive; he only cares for his own safety, his own pleasures, and his own power.

---

[1]Foakes, op. cit., lvi ff.

Wilson Knight in his ecstatic manner finds in *Henry VIII* the culminating point in Shakespeare's work: '*Henry VIII* binds and clasps this massive life-work into a single whole expanding the habitual design of Shakespearian tragedy: from normality, through a violent conflict to a spiritualized music, and thence to the concluding ritual'.[1] On Knight's 'interpretation', which is full of exuberance of sentiment and extravagance in expression, the significance of the play lies primarily in the concluding ritual and in Cranmer's prophecy, which, in forecasting the triumphs of two reigns, defines the indwelling spirit of the nation. The defect of this view is that it places emphasis on what lies quite outside the drama, which, even if it contains a philosophy, must express it through action and character. What happened during the reigns of Elizabeth and James I is unrelated to the plot of *Henry VIII*, and the ritual of baptism ends a drama rather than begins one. Cranmer is certainly a pious Christian, but the influence he exercises on the course of events is very negligible indeed. As the King has made up his mind about Katharine even before the Black-Friars trial, Cranmer comes back to England from his foreign mission only to confirm what his master has already decided on. And Wolsey's example is there to show what fate would have overtaken this well-beloved servant if he had thrown any obstacle in the King's path. The 'spiritualized music' which Wilson Knight finds in Cranmer's ritual and his prophecy is a critical deduction rather than an organic part of the dramatic action.

From the Prologue it appears that *Henry VIII* was designed as a story of the fall of princes, not, as in Boccaccio and Lydgate, of persons of remote antiquity but of people who lived not far off from the time of the dramatist and his audience. There *is* unity in the theme, for Buckingham, Wolsey, and Katharine were mighty people who came to a sad end. But there is variety also, for Buckingham is the victim of intrigue and Katharine of untoward circumstances, whereas Wolsey was ruined by ambition – 'By that sin fell the angels'. The drama records the rise of some persons as it reviews the decline of others. Not only is there contrast in fortunes but there is a good deal of difference between the protagonists of the various episodes. Wolsey is insolent and ambitious, and a man who gave the clergy ill example, being of his own body ill, but Cranmer is humble, pious, and chaste.

[1] *The Crown of Life*, p. 326.

Katharine might have been a sweet bed-fellow, but she is old, and her husband is tired of her – 'hates' is Katharine's own word – whereas Anne is young and fascinating, and the King is desperately in love with her. The play has been called more a piece of pageantry than a drama, but the pageantry is not without dramatic significance. It shows the passing away of an old order and the birth of a new, and it is in this context that Cranmer's baptismal speech becomes dramatically relevant. It is from this point of view, again, that Henry, a lustful, capricious and selfish prince, finds his appropriate place in the emergence of the new order. He was originally a tool in the hands of Wolsey whose power seemed to be unlimited. Although at the insistence of his wife he redresses the grievances of the clothiers, he cannot know how his crafty minister would turn the concession to his own advantage. But gradually he rises to his full stature as king; he sees through the delaying tactics of Rome and dismisses Wolsey without pity and without regret. His selfishness has thus its nobler side. It helps him to get out of Wolsey's leading strings, and to free England from the shackles of Rome. When he refuses to show any mercy to Buckingham, he is a tool in the hands of Wolsey; when he casts away Wolsey, he acts on his own initiative and in his own interests, but he is also assisted by the active support of the nobles who hate Wolsey and of the Commons flayed by Wolsey's taxes. But when he saves Cranmer, he is alone; not even the Dukes of Suffolk and Norfolk are in his confidence. When, later on, he says at the end of Cranmer's great speech,

> O lord archbishop!
> Thou hast made me now a man,
>
> (V. v. 64–65)

his words have a deeper meaning than he is himself aware of. The course of the drama shows the development of the King's personality, and it is this development that helps to bind the scattered threads of the story; but the deeper unity is thematic rather than personal. Life is portrayed as a flowing stream; the current at one point may be different from what it was or what it will be, but in spite of the devious paths it may take, it is a unity, for the simple reason that its essence is ceaseless movement. Nothing is real in life except its continuous flow:

Of Life only there is no end; and though of its million starry mansions many are empty and many still unbuilt, and though its vast domain is still unbearably desert, my seed shall one day fill it and master its matter to its uttermost confines. And for what may be beyond, the eyesight of Lilith is too short. It is enough that there is a beyond.

(Bernard Shaw : *Back To Methuselah*)

It is this lesson about the continuity of life's movement that links *Henry VIII* to Shakespeare's other historical plays.

Index